I0542898

TO TELL THE
TRUTH
THE AGE OF MIND

FRED L FOX

Inquiries and Book Orders should be addressed to:

Great Writers Media
Email: info@greatwritersmedia.com
Phone: 877-600-5469

ISBN: 978-1-961416-11-6 (sc)
ISBN: 978-1-961416-12-3 (ebk)

CONTENTS

Part Three - The Age Of Mind

PREFACE
A PERSPECTIVE

Have you ever felt that life could be better? Is yours really all that you want it to be? If your answers are *yes* and *no* in that order, this is your book.

This book is all about *you* and making your life better. Making it all you want it to be will require some input from you, but what you read here will give you a running start.

Your task is complicated by a world fraught with problems, some of which are so common that we accept them without even thinking of them as obstacles to a better life. Our attitude toward truth is an example. We tend to be indifferent toward equivocation, duplicity, deceit, even outright lies, often excusing the deceiver out of hand. We even redefine the term to make it better fit the situation. After all, what can you do? It's just the way it goes. Live with it.

The problem is that the malady spreads as people become inured to it. Things get worse. And that's what's happened. There's a general lack of trust and wide disagreement about what ought to be done to fix it and solving the wrong problem(s) can make matters worse. How bad can it get? We're witnessing it. And you don't have to live with it.

To Tell The Truth... isolates the issues, identifies the problems and their causes, and offers a simple, practical and effective solution *that works.* Correctly identified, our societal problems are so fundamental that their solutions turn out to be fundamental as well. Going on that assumption, we start with fundamentals: First Principles and the individual...*you.*

Anything of substance has to be built on a solid foundation, and First Principles provide the foundation for this book. These basic foundational axioms— knowns, givens, absolutes—can't be inferred from any other proposition or assumption. They just *are*—-put simply, *what is,* and **truth,** the principal Principle, provides the backbone of this book.

While our problems are social, their solutions rest with the individual, and that means *you.* The solution proposed here is systemic; it cannot fail. And if you heed the message, neither can you. Your life *will* be better. And your life is, really, all about **you.**

> *This is the final edition of To Tell*
> *The Truth. It's been a trip...*

INTRODUCTION

You are the most important person in your life. But who *are* you, really? Well, who you are is what you do with what you are—the gender, race, and distinctive physical makeup you were born with: male, female, black, white, tall, short, whatever, a totally unique human being in the same world with countless other totally unique human beings, each with a brain weighing in the neighborhood of three pounds and the same universal truths to work with. You breathe air and your heart pumps blood. Gravity works as well for you as for anyone else. Your day is the same length. You have feelings and emotions. You can form or quit relationships. Just like everyone else.

But you—the who you are—are *not* just like everyone else. Who you are is entirely unique to you and what you do with the virtually limitless resources available to you. The fact is that you have within yourself a storehouse of life knowledge courtesy of your three-pound brain, which also provides access to the entire wisdom of humanity. Everyone starts with the same resources, but not everyone is aware of them. Those who are aware handle them in their own unique fashion. How you handle them determines who you are.

While you can't control *what* you are, you have the power to be whoever you want to be. Just unlock your mind to what's already there and believe what you already know, and you will become all you can be.

It's very straightforward; simply apply the facts of life starting with the principal one—the one that's been redefined to the point of pointlessness as our society has plunged into the future—*truth.*

It's this book's task to put truth into sharp focus using common knowledge uncommonly dealt with, and approach essential issues from an honest perspective. And it's really quite simple. Just trust in yourself and *what is*, and you will become all that you really are.

People who study these things tell us that the written word can handle about 30-percent of personal communication. But effective communication requires more. Speaking adds *tone*, increasing effectiveness by another 10-15%. But often even that's not enough to clearly relate exactly what's meant. Concepts and feelings are difficult to transmit because we *think* and, as subjective beings, we each think individually. Also, what one person says may not be what another hears, which may not be what the speaker means.

You'll notice that we've used *italics* to provide some degree of *tone* and **bolding** to emphasize certain important points in an effort to increase understanding. While this may slow down the reader to some extent, the object of this book is to cause you to *think* and reflect, and this ought to be a positive feature rather than a negative one. We trust that it will help drive home the important points.

PART ONE

It's All About You

CHAPTER ONE

Vital Relationships and What You Already Know

Do you realize how important you are? Well, think about it and you'll appreciate that you are the only *you* who ever was or will be. That makes you special because you, the individual, are the basic building block of humanity. Your reaction to anything that happens will be unique for all time, so everything you do must be special in some way, even if you don't agree with it, care about it or understand it. Nobody else will ever see through *your* eyes, or ever have *your* unique imagination or intuition. Nobody else will ever understand things exactly as you do. You're one-of-a-kind—-forever, and what you do will affect others. Forever. That's power. Why not make it a positive force for humanity and make your own life better at the same time?

Who are you? What are you? Why are you? Well, you're already knocking at the door of higher philosophy. We'll get to that, but for now we'll deal with the *what* of you.

You already know that you're unique and some part, however large or small, of "the big picture." You can also come up with descriptive verbiage that will help define you in as much detail as you wish. But be careful! Remember that right now you're only dealing with your *self.* Nobody else, no relationship, no group, counts, so you can't define yourself in terms of others and especially not in terms of any group of which you may be a part.

But what you are came into this air-breathing world with a surplus of brain cells and sufficient other raw materials to become a significant member of humanity. What you are, including your basic physical and emotional makeup, is really a function of history, a product of the past (but not your past). Whatever you are is what you've been given.

You are a part of the big picture like it or not, so the big picture is not truly complete without you. You make it what it is simply by being, and your particular piece of the puzzle just might be one of the more important parts. That's why you're here in the first place. The importance of this statement cannot be overemphasized. Your importance cannot be overemphasized. So while you're here, make it count.

Within the context of mankind, the individual (you) has no limits. You're connected and unable to sever your fundamental bond with mankind because your freedom, independence and continuance exist totally within its constraints. You also cannot presume to be independent of other individuals; their humanity is their basic bond. Each unique individual is an equally vital and viable entity that cannot *be* entirely on his own. You are what you are. All you have to do is *be* who you are.

One person alone can accomplish only so much, and whatever that might be can't survive without relationships. It's just another given that we have to deal with; avoid or in some way relate to others, each as unique as we are. (In fact, we can only complete ourselves in others.)

A final word about the power of one: without *one* there would be no computers; these run—simply—on the power of one and *nothing*—zero. Ones and zeroes, that's *it*. More about this later. In the meantime, don't be a zero.

Relationships

Sooner or later you'll connect with another person based on a mutual need, interest or goal, thereby creating a third party; a collective entity, a mutual vitality, the sum of which is greater than its parts. This phenomenon ($1 + 1 > 2$) is the reason for humanity's persistent progress.

Our *selfs* are what make us special, and since your self is nothing less than the source of energy for the progression of humanity, you are responsible to humanity for maintaining your individuality. This is important! It helps if you know yourself thoroughly, but remember that you are, after all, no more or less an individual than the rest of us.

But individuals may forget their fundamental bond with humanity and that without others they could not *be*, let alone survive or progress. They may see themselves as inferior or superior to others or worse yet, independent of them.

In order to live right and live fully, all you really have to do is accept responsibility for yourself and allow others to do the same. If you did nothing more, humanity would move forward just as it did before you and will after you.

Without mankind, the individual has no meaning, but within the context of mankind, the individual has no limits. You cannot sever your fundamental bond with mankind because your being, freedom and continuance exist only within its constraints. Nor can you presume to be independent of others; humanity is the basic bond between individuals. Each unique individual is an equally vital and viable entity that cannot *be* entirely on his or her own. In fact, connection is essential and inevitable.

As soon as individuals connect, progression happens. Progression is inevitable. Mankind is doomed to progress. The only alternative to progression is humanity's demise.

As you progress, you become. And since you will connect, you will inevitably deal with others. This will be discussed in considerable detail later, but first, let's begin with...

The Way We *Think* It Is

We've been aboard Planet Earth for untold thousands of years. We've picked up considerable information along the way and we've learned a lot. You'd think that by this time we'd have a pretty good handle on the way things are.

And, in fact, we do. But you've read this before, now read it again:

Your *self* is nothing less than the source of energy for the progression of humanity; you are responsible to humanity for maintaining your individuality.

Our ready acceptance of the complex seduces us into ignoring the simple. We're jaded by dizzying scientific progress: computers, nuclear power, rocket science, global communication, space stations. Microchips the size of a baby's fingernail do our calculating and much of our thinking; they fly our planes and tune our engines even as they're running. And this progress continues at an ever-increasing rate. We are, in fact, stunned by it. And frankly, we can't handle it all.

So we delegate responsibility for progress to those who seem better prepared to handle the task of moving us forward in the giant steps to which we've become accustomed. This severely limits our options. We're not using the most important resources at our disposal: our *selves.*

We've effectively signed over our individual creativity and ingenuity to others. We've given them permission to tell us what to think. We accept what they tell us as the way it is. By thus limiting ourselves, we avoid using every available resource. Often there's more than one way to reach a goal, and the shortest route may not be the best. Further, not reaching that goal does not mean failure if we learn from what we've done along the way.

The following example illustrates a couple of problems: What is this?

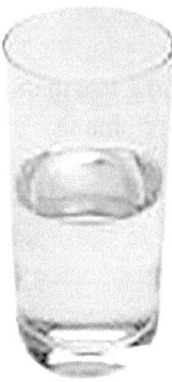

One answer is, in the vernacular, a half glass of water.

You can make a more refined interpretation that puts the answer (and so the question as well) on yet another level. You may think that there's more to the question than there appears to be, that your answer must have some deeper significance by perceiving the glass as half full, or half empty. Or the wrong size. Again, not wise.

Instead of sharpening the focus, this approach clouds it. The question is, simply, "What *is* this?" Not "What does this mean to you?" It's really just a glass with about half its volume occupied, probably by water. But say a half glass of water, and almost everyone will know what you mean. Usually.

This example illustrates both definition and perception—what's seen (or heard) as opposed to what's meant—not to mention the meaning of words. It's easy to convey a simple meaning, but it's equally easy to confuse the issue by reading more into a simple question than is intended.

If we hope to get where we have to be, we have to get on track and remain there. We have to make certain that we're all talking about and hearing the same thing— what's meant. That's what communication is all about.

The concepts described in this book are basic, maybe even simplistic, but why make things complicated when they're not?

An Exercise

We live in a world of infinitely varying shades of color, including grays. Sometimes we forget black and white, which by the way are not opposites like right/wrong, left/right, up/down, good/bad.

Consider the following simple exercise. Feel free to fill in as many blanks as you wish; use additional paper if necessary.

BLACK	WHITE
OFF	ON
FALSE	TRUE
IMPOSSIBLE	POSSIBLE
==========	==========
-----------------	-----------------
-----------------	-----------------

You'll notice that these are not just opposites. They are absolutes. White *is* (color), black *isn't* (it's the absence of color). Truth *is*, false is truth's absence. Heat *is*, cold is the absence of heat. Possible *is*, impossible *isn't*. On *is*, off *isn't*. *Absolutes.* Be careful to differentiate these from mere opposites like left and right. Absolutes are givens.

Knowing that things can be pretty good, not bad, or partially correct doesn't change the fact that an electric current is what it is only so long as it's *on*. When it's *off*, it simply does not exist—it *isn't*. That's an absolute truth, a given.

In spite of what we may think or have been led to believe, there are certain virtually timeless givens. Time itself, gravity, light and progression are givens that apply to everyone, every time. Not only will the sun "rise" in the east and "set" in the west tomorrow, you can bet your life on exactly where and when it will do so. The stars, moon and tides are on an absolute schedule over which we have absolutely no control. You can absolutely count on these things. They operate without our approval or need to explain them. Accept them. Because you *must*.

In spite of our vast collective knowledge, we don't even know for certain what's possible, or what's not. (Clearly some things are impossible, such as that electric current being at the same time on and off.) We can say with certainty, however, that **everything except the impossible is possible**, even if we don't really know exactly what that means.

But how can we presume to know what is, and what isn't? Well, we can start with those things we can count on. Absolutes. Givens.

The Way Things Might Be

Things might not be perfect in this imperfect world, but you'll probably agree that some could be better than they are. The difference is just a matter of degree. I say we can get much closer to perfection than we're willing to admit, and this book suggests how to do it. You simply have to accept truth and reject all else. Easy? Not quite.

But if you want to see real progress, start with the resources at your disposal! And before you head for Google or the library, consider the mirror.

Consider what you already know and count on— those givens, such as the fact that the tides advance and retreat, that your heart beats without your directing it, that you breathe in spite of yourself, that when you drop something it usually falls to the ground. This simple exercise can get you a lot of useful and true information— *knowledge*—fast. The only requirement is that you believe what you already know. And don't ignore your intuition on the grounds that it can't be proven. What if it's right? (Look it up and see that it usually is). And if it's right, why waste time proving what you already know? Take the givens—they're absolutely free—and trust them. You can always trust *what is* (truth).

Now consider your imagination. In our advanced state of sophistication we forget the delight of discovering simple things that children enjoy on a daily basis.

Now, *think!* Almost anyone can do it. But think, don't just reprise.

For instance, the something/nothing relationship of binary math and, not incidentally, the most sophisticated of computers, hinges on that simple model:

$$0 = \text{off} = \textit{no}\text{thing}; \ 1 = \text{on} = \textit{some}\text{thing}$$

Off/on is all it takes. Without that simple concept, none of what follows can happen, yet most of us pass right over this reality without fully appreciating it, marveling instead at the powerful machine that it enables.

It doesn't get much simpler than black and white, or on and off. Yet we fail to consider the implications of these conditions, convinced that nothing's really black or white but instead one of 256 shades of grey. You can't make a bigger mistake.

Don't ignore the basics or the givens. That's where you start when you need to be absolutely sure that you're on solid ground. And solid ground is where we've got to be.

Now that you have some real knowledge, consider what's available to process it…

Your Brain

Maybe you believe that heavy thinking is best done by those trained for it, and you may be right. Or you might want to leave it to others because you have better things to do, and that may be fitting. But you can't slough off the thinking process onto others for lack of raw materials on your part.

You share with the rest of the human races the most well-developed three-pound organ ever evolved, and the software to run it—mind. These are givens. You can count on it. If you couldn't, you couldn't count at all. Accept the fact and apply it.

It's been estimated that most of us use less than 10-percent of our brain— some estimates are as low as 3-4%. Assume for a moment that this is true (we can't *know* it). Ever wonder what's in the rest, or even why it's there?

Well, it's not there to take up space, and it's not a stockpile. It's there because it *was* needed. If it weren't needed it wouldn't have evolved, because evolution is the process of development of an organism to adapt and survive in response to outside forces. We don't just grow brains because we may need them some day. We either have all the brain we need *or* less than the brain needed earlier (give that a second thought); the whole three pounds has or had a function. If we seem to use only about five ounces of it, why do we have the rest? And what's in it? Could it contain in excess of 10-20 times as much data, information, knowledge or processing power as we're now using? I don't know. Nor do you.

And your brain, for all practical purposes, is just as large and complex as anyone else's, including any known rocket scientist's, give or take an ounce or two. You own the raw materials to solve any problem that anyone else can solve. In fact, as far as you are concerned, you can solve that problem better than anyone else can. Think about that.

How smart are you, anyway? Well, you might not be a genius, but it's not required that you or anyone else *be* one. Not necessary, not expected, and not likely. But if brainpower is any criterion, you may be at least ten times smarter than you think you are, even by the most modest estimate.

And since geniuses aren't perfect either, not being one doesn't in any way make you inferior. We all have unique variations that make us exceptional and able to perform in different ways. Stratospheric IQs may be one of them, but so are physical strength, coordination, tolerance and countless other attributes necessary to the development of the species, including "common sense," whatever you may define that to be. Nobody has it all. Mankind operates at many levels, and thought achieves quite different results at different levels. The combination is awesome, and it's the combination that matters to humanity. And you are integral to humanity. In fact, you *are* humanity—in person.

Because you can't be perfect is no reason to settle for what rolls your way. There's lots of room for improvement. It's up to you how far you want to take it, and that's what determines how smart you are.

Easy to say, but not so easy to do, because we've given others permission to tell us what to think, accepting what they tell us as the way it is. We've been *led to believe*, and by thus limiting ourselves, we avoid using every available resource including ourselves. Believe this: You are your most valuable resource. And one reason for this is that you are a given. You are "for real".

The rapid progress of knowledge and technology encourages us to delegate responsibility to those who seem better prepared to handle it. It's an easy mistake to make. While it's natural, it severely limits our options.

You, The Individual

In the case of the human race*s*, it takes one each, male and female, to create a new individual self. Existence of that self requires that it be physically cut loose, perhaps even forced to take its first breath, and nurtured for some period of time. It's not possible for an individual to be conceived, born and survive without others, and if those others choose to reject him, he's done for. This makes a connection with at least one other as fundamental as the individual himself and, since bonds work both ways, the other(s) must have a vital connection with each member as well. Mutual vitality is more than an important concept. It's a given.

Some kind of family–a blood kindred–is directly responsible for a person's conception and birth, and to whom the individual is in permanent debt. *Family is the primary source of being.*

Once survival is established, the next step is progression, or growth, or development, or whatever you wish to call moving on. Like the path from conception to survival, the step from survival to progression is involuntary on our part–it simply happens to us. How far it proceeds depends on who's involved, but once survival is accomplished the level of living increases.

The point here is that conception and survival occur without the conscious effort of the individual, and progression happens without any conscious effort as well. These things are automatic—you are a function of them. As far as you are concerned, they are givens, and that makes you a given as well.

As you become, you progress. And since you will connect, you will inevitably deal with others.

There are other combinations of individuals that most certainly are vital and necessary to life and living—clans, tribes and community among them. All these tend to be self-supportive, sharing responsibilities, perhaps even possessions. Clans and tribes tend to be familial, related in some way by blood and/or ethnicity. Community, on the other hand, is a larger, but still closely-knit, assemblage of people with a common background which often goes beyond family or ethnicity. To keep things simple, we will deal here only with community.

Beyond The Self - Community

The phenomenon of connection discussed earlier is the basis and substance of community. In fact, the mutual vitality created by the personal connection of two individuals is a principle of community. Another is interdependence, and still another is responsibility; more is written later about both of these principles.

Initial development of the individual happens within his family. Beyond that the person's association expands to an extended family such as a clan, tribe or community. These are not groups, which are formed to satisfy a particular need or desire, but represent the social setting where the person develops as a human being—where he becomes.

Nor are communities formed so much as they become, establishing themselves to satisfy vital (life-supporting) needs. Community is built on the reciprocally personal relationship of individuals arising out of some vital bond like blood, ethnicity or heritage—something related to the person, not an institution. The distinction is made on the merits of personal bonding rather than a societal or group relationship. Community often augments the functions of the family, taking on responsibility (even accountability) for the individual's survival.

However, the vital connection necessary for community implies that any rules set by a community be in accord with moral (not legal) principle; therefore, *True community is fundamentally ethical,* whereas the group need not be.

This is not splitting hairs. To understand life and its meaning, it's necessary to distinguish between relationships that are vital and those that are not.

The individual's education originates with the family and community at the moral/ethical level. This is where individuals are exposed to others with whom they must coexist and upon whom they must depend. Community reinforces, even extends, the family's ability to foster the extension and progression of the individual, and strengthens his link to the whole of humanity (and therefore his access to its collective knowledge).

Community encourages the free exchange of ideas, betterment and growth. Community grows—becomes—by the power of the multiple combined strengths and trust of the various individuals comprising it, not on the basis of getting something done.

Before we leave our discussion of community, there is one thing we ought to add: the necessity for trust. Consider the following allegory.

A pilot takes off at night in a small airplane, flies entirely in clouds for hundreds of miles, comes out of the clouds a few feet above the runway of choice and lands safely at his destination without ever seeing beyond his instrument panel. He does this using standard equipment already in the plane, a passive navigation system already in place, and one other vitally important element.

Neither the airplane nor its instruments are complex. They operate on simple physical principles (givens) available to anyone, but without his instruments our pilot couldn't even maintain the aircraft in a level attitude for more than a short time, let alone move in the right direction at a safe altitude. Chances of landing anywhere safely would be all but non-existent, and getting to his destination virtually impossible.

Part of the in-place navigation system comes with the earth: gravity, the earth's magnetic field and its atmosphere (givens, indeed). A simple compass permits our pilot to at least head in the right direction and differences in air density provide altitude information. But winds and other natural phenomena will alter his course and mountains and other hard objects may preclude his getting back on the ground safely. These problems are handled by a world-wide network of precision navigation aids (based, of course, on givens) operating silently day and night. Our pilot's instruments tell him precisely where his airplane is and at what altitude, exactly where the runway is and even the approach necessary to land safely.

None of this requires the active participation of anyone else. Our pilot, alone, stands an excellent chance of getting to where he's going. To do this, he has to have knowledge of the systems that are operating as well as that other vital element: *confidence in those systems and himself.* He has to know and *trust* those systems that work no matter what he does, and he has to trust in his instruments, no matter what.

The point is this: without that one other important element–knowledge of and trust in his equipment and those timeless givens that operate even when (or even if) he does not–our pilot hasn't a chance.

The point is this: *trust* yourself and the unseen, unknown and unproven systems that work even if you do not—the givens. Why question *what is*? Accept it.

Community, in fact, is founded in trust rather than the law. It cannot survive without it because its members are connected intimately by their humanity. Their very survival depends on *trust*. And so does yours.

CHAPTER TWO

The Group
Group Relationships and
Their Inherent Problems

L ife-centered concepts deal with being and becoming. Group-centered concepts deal with getting things done. While social, public and community groups, institutions, government and the like may be inevitable, none are individually vital.

The Group Is Not A Vital Entity

The individual, family, true community and humanity are vital—living— elements of civilization; therefore, relationships within and between them are vital as well. In contrast, the group relationship is not vital. It is transient—a temporary response to some current interest of individuals to get something done.

Individuals seek out (or form) a group for various reasons including stimulation, survival, problem-solving, competition, to make life easier, good feelings, or maybe just a sense of belonging. Conversely, a group may seek out individuals to increase its own authority, power or effectiveness.

While individuals may contribute something unique to a group, at the same time they will trade some part of themselves for group benefits. But the lure of perceived group benefits may seduce them into giving up too much. Don't make the mistake of thinking of yourself or anyone else only in the context of a group. The group can't give you vital rights—you already have them. With your life and individuality, you are everything because you are vital.

Some groups may be small, others very large. All are formed by individuals toward some end—social, athletic, religious, political, academic, educational, entertainment, criminal, environmental, governmental, whatever.

While it's possible for a group to emulate community, bonds must become personal rather than institutional. This is by no means a common occurrence.

Groups include organizations, institutions and other aggregations of individuals brought together to get things done. They may be useful and even inevitable, but they're not vital to humanity. Following are some examples:

It's the nature of groups to deal with special interests. A vital connection, a personal bond such as blood or heritage, something basic to the person rather than the group, is not required. Groups organize to get things done. This makes group relationships distinctly different from vital ones. They are expendable. They are temporary. The difference is critical.

While groups may provide protection, reflection and synergy, it's the members who provide the ideas and creativity for things to happen. Groups may accelerate the process but they can't initiate it; only living beings can do that. The group is not a living thing, but it may give the impression that it *is*, and its members may make the all-too-common mistake of believing it.

Groups may give the appearance of personal bonding by design or assertion (some institutions such as churches, governments, teams, survive on this basis). Nevertheless, it remains true that groups are not permanent. When a group begins to exist for itself, seeking power or permanence rather than the cause for which it was organized, then even the most exemplary of groups oversteps its bounds and threatens the individual, mankind, or both. (This *dilemma of the group* is discussed in some detail later).

The What and Why Of Groups

The earliest relationships are formed by individuals dependent upon each other for their very existence, the most basic of which is of course the family. Next in order is the extended family, tribe or community that contributes to each member's survival and growth. These represent vital relationships.

While community retains vital relationships, it also provides fertile ground for the development of group phenomena as it grows. Members of a community can be attracted to each other for many reasons. As these earliest relationships grow in strength and number, survival becomes less of an issue, and improving their lot, more. People learn, teach and progress, growing into larger and more productive cultures, and as they do they are able to pursue more personal avenues of interest—to specialize more and more as individuals. As interest moves beyond survival to include personal and end-centered factors, groups are formed. This growth and specialization is characteristic of civilization.

Groups have assumed greater importance as civilization has progressed (and are in fact a contributing factor in that progression). They get many things done faster and often better than a family or community could because they are able to concentrate their efforts on the task at hand rather than deal with all the complex functions necessary to the individual and the whole of mankind. In one way or another, groups *specialize*. In order to improve upon what they would do, groups develop systems that enable them to operate more efficiently in their efforts to accomplish their particular ends.

However, in so doing, something often is lost. In gearing up for efficiency to get something done, some part of the vital relationship may be sacrificed. Individual wants and needs usually are subjugated in some degree to those of the group, and often even individual responsibility is sacrificed to the group.

Even though group rules may infringe to some degree on their members, some individuals choose to subscribe to them in the cause of accomplishment. It's the same with any group, small or large, and it's important to realize that even our society is nothing but a very large group—a "supergroup", if you will. It's equally important to realize that in spite of its size our society is still smaller than (and therefore subservient to) the whole of humanity, and that it may not supersede any individual's personal vital link with humanity.

Groups often assume more importance than they really have, affecting in a very real way the relationships between individuals. The progression goes as follows.

Evolution Of The Group

It takes considerable time and energy to learn all you need to know to become tops in your field, or to collect the knowledge necessary to develop a new product, or to break out of the mold into a new way of thinking. To pursue a particular interest to the highest level, something usually is compromised, something that may be important to us as humans but that we choose to sacrifice as we persist in the interest of getting something done.

In our drive to do it all and do it now, we've spawned an elite of experts—*specialists*—who expend some part of their individuality to achieve some goal. You may number among them.

Experts attain their level of expertise through education, experience and critical thinking. But more appropriate to this discussion, they tend to gather together into groups with others who have the same interest in order to get something done.

Experts collaborate with others working in the same specialty, stimulated by interaction and challenged by their peers. They may pour their very life into their work in order to advance the state of their particular endeavor. The effort may be altruistic, commercial or selfish, and results may or may not be worthwhile, but often the fruits of their labors benefit mankind in some way, large or small.

But at the end of the day, most of these specialists leave their group and return to family or community to renew their link with humanity and its collective purpose.

Most specialists and experts operate in the context of the group only to get something done, then leave the group to recharge their batteries. While their group may develop a "life" of its own, it's not a whole life because it's not vital. Its purpose is to provide a channel for the creative power of the individual, improve a product, increase the clout of the group or further the power of individuals within it. (If it were to somehow provide a total environment, it would be in danger (?!) of becoming a community.)

Many groups including the supergroup of our society reward experts with higher status and greater compensation than the man on the street. While this status within the group may be earned, it doesn't extend beyond the group. Regardless of how high a person rises within any group (or even the supergroup itself), that person remains an equal and integral part of humanity no more or less than any other individual. We are at the same time endowed with and condemned to the non-issue of equality (more about this following). Status within any group, however large and powerful, is not directly transferable to humanity.

But when many expert-specialists leave their group to renew their vital link, they take their status with them and apply it liberally to the point of domination of other areas of their lives and the lives of others with whom they come in contact.

Our society and its laws facilitate this phenomenon. Experts, authorities, specialists, entertainers, government officials, athletes, even weather reporters and other "personalities" in highly visible fields often are afforded importance all out of proportion to that which they warrant as human beings. We tend to accept this because somehow, "important" people seem larger than life and better prepared than the average person to move humanity forward in the giant steps to which we've become accustomed. But even worse, we may assign to them many of the responsibilities we could handle better ourselves, simply because of their higher profile. And we've done just that.

Take for example medicine, law and higher education, callings usually requiring advanced degrees and considerable investment of time and financial resources. Individuals in these fields join together in what have become powerful and dynamic groups that benefit and compel the respect of society and those with lesser "professional" status. But often, key individuals within these groups are sought out as authorities beyond their areas of expertise. The same may be true of rock stars, actors, politicians, even meteorologists. Wealth or notoriety alone may be sufficient to justify their opinions in politics and public discourse. While the rich and famous may be at the top of their own fields, there's no reason to assume or accept their influence beyond those fields. They in fact may have no expertise to offer beyond their fame.

All might be well if these individuals honestly aim to serve humanity and act morally. Some do. However, unless their authority is tempered with responsibility, it's all too easy for them to become answerable only to themselves and their group(s). When this happens, the system that we have created overpowers us. You should know that the tail is now wagging the dog, and it started happening long ago.

And The Results

We have, over the course of time, effectively subverted the natural process in the name of the way we think (or have been led to believe) that things are. The rapid growth of knowledge and technology has encouraged us to form groups to get things done. In the process we have effectively signed over much of our own creativity, imagination and ingenuity to others, giving *them* permission to tell us what to think and accepting what *they* tell us as the way it is. We have become caught up in self-interest and ignored our vital link with humanity. In the process we have drawn further from the principle, the reason for it all—*to be, to live, to create, to become all that we can be*—what life itself is all about. We forget that the vital connection includes more than shared interests and abilities. It includes, in fact, everything that makes us human, and it begins with that First Principle, *truth*.

When life was simpler, when family and community were critical to our very survival, the link with humanity was obvious if not fully exploited. As things progressed and information burgeoned we tended to connect with others in groups with similar interests and abilities. The group connection, with its challenges, rewards and even sheer enjoyment, became pervasive. Even so, there would be no negative aspects of this phenomenon if we maintained and nourished our vital link with humanity.

But as we developed stronger and stronger group connections we also developed, group by group, a system of laws that has tended to mask our vital link with humanity. We tended to forget that even our society, arguably the high-water mark of mankind, is still a group, and as a group it's disposable. We tended to forget that humankind remains the vital and overarching entity to which we are vitally connected. We tended to forget that groups, however large and pervasive, do not and cannot replace the individual, family, or community, no matter what we're told or what we've come to believe.

When we permitted group relationships to displace the vital ones in importance, we allowed groups (including society itself) to appropriate greater authority, and some members greater influence, than they are due. In this process, group rules corrupt the basic ethical precepts of mankind. Groups have written their own rules to accomplish their own ends, and these rules have found their way into law that may (and often does) misrepresent the relationship between the group and the individual. We have allowed, even encouraged, this to happen, and in the process we've subverted ethics in favor of law (group think) by assigning our own ethical responsibilities to groups that by definition cannot handle them.

The effect has been devastating on both levels that really matter: the individual and the whole of mankind. Should this trend be allowed to play itself out, total destruction of our society would be imminent.

Fortunately this trend cannot play itself out. It is not within any group's power to own mankind, because big as the biggest group may be, it's neither vital nor a given and, in the final analysis, even the least of givens will prevail over any group. And never forget that *you* are a given. The least of us, you included, can prevail if we so choose.

In fact, humanity can and will save us from ourselves. As an ethical whole, humanity will overcome any group effort to destroy it, because ethics does not go away. Givens are absolute.

The current degenerative trend can be reversed at any time simply by reverting to truth. Anyone, including you, can do it. The individual's relationship to any group never has been vital to his existence. Any relationship with any group may be severed without permanent damage to the individual or mankind generally.

It's a natural inclination to become engrossed in one's own work and relate only to others who understand and approve of what we're doing, while disregarding other aspects of our own lives and those of others. We all have to guard against this inclination for we all are experts and specialists in our own right. Each of us is totally unique, and each of us is equally and totally responsible.

Illustrating The Group Dilemma – The Law

Positive law (law that is posited—assumed) is the system of laws by which our society is governed. Devised for the purpose of regulating behavior in and of itself, it is *of* society, serves the purposes of society and may be modified as purposes of our society change.

We've correctly noted that the major challenge to right living comes from resolving relationships. A conflict here stems from that function of law dealing with relationships, an area where law and morality appear to intersect, but where they actually overlap in different planes. Morality applies to *everyone* (i.e., the entirety of humanity, where equality, for instance, is not an issue), while positive law applies only to the group that posits it. This law must deal with institutional relationships—those relationships within the group to which the law applies—but it has no function with regard to personal–vital–ones. When any group (including society) applies its laws to vital relationships, it creates problems that it can't resolve. It has done just that with respect to equality.

Equality

Our laws are supposed to advocate justice, and perhaps they do. But examine the word *just*. It implies honesty, morality, fairness and impartiality, among other things, and while the law proclaims these virtues, it cannot always employ them. What positive law does is to ensure due process. This means only that it must follow the rule of law, its own law, which may be whatever the society that makes it, wishes. The law must make concessions in order to accomplish what it claims to seek—"the greatest good for the greatest number." The law must *judge*. Perhaps this is justified (and please note that justified can mean *excused* as well as *proven,* illustrating again how words can cloud meaning and showing the very real ambiguity of the law).

The foregoing illustrates both the law's ambiguity and its ethical status. The law operates on legal, not ethical, principle. This probably is as it should be. After all, we can't always operate on the basis of perfection because none of us are perfect. How then can our law be perfect? Obviously it cannot and is not, *nor should we be expected to honor its definition of ethics or ethical verities like equality.*

An example of problems caused by a group's operating beyond its limits is illustrated by the issue of *equality.* We're all familiar with the following:

"ALL MEN ARE CREATED EQUAL"

It's true and, as a given, there's no ethical problem here. The problem lies in trying to define abstract terms (like truth) using group rules—laws.

Of course, the group may redefine equality according to its own rules to mean anything it wishes, but its definition can only be in the context of that particular group and can't be extended beyond it. The basic definition *must* remain intact.

True equality extends beyond any group, so the group runs out of territory when trying to deal with the term. Real equality can't be given because we already have it. It's simply not a social issue.

And any group making it an issue goes beyond its limits. *All men are created equal, and at the same time each is unique and develops uniquely, while remaining at all times equal.* Few, if any, institutions can deal with this.

Positive Law and Equality

The differences between societal law and morality are as marked as the differences between the group and humankind. Morality means principle, virtue, probity, not law. (Positive) law means decree, legislation, ruling, not morality.

Law may descend from moral principle (ethics) but the process is neither automatic nor reversible. On the other hand, moral principle does not require the law for validation—moral principle simply *is*. Law that seeks to be universal not only requires morality for validation but presupposes it.

So long as society remains a group, our laws will not—cannot—be entirely ethical in spite of what society claims.

A simple illustration: We are sworn to tell "the truth, the whole truth and nothing but..." But are we? While the prosecution must hew to the truth in proving its case against the criminal, neither the accused nor his advocate must follow suit. The criminal is, in effect and *in fact*, expected to lie, or at least not to tell "the *whole* truth," and his attorney is presumed to support his case. After all, whether or not he *is* guilty, criminal law says that a criminal must be proven guilty, even offering protection against self-incrimination. If a guilty person always told the truth (i.e., were ethical), the function of the court would be limited to sentencing and punishment. A nice idea, but that's not the way it is.

A simple question makes the point: Where is equality in all this? We certainly aren't equal under the law if some must tell the truth (be ethical) while others need not do so.

Affording positive law ethical status is intellectually dishonest. In the final analysis, institutional law may benefit the institution, but unless it is completely ethical, it will fail at least some individuals, and therefore humanity.

Ethics will never—cannot—fail either individual *or* humanity. If it should fail a group, the problem lies with the group.

So despite our society's claims, we are not all equal under its law. We are, in fact, equal *before* the law. Equality is a perfect and unambiguous ethical concept. The law is imperfect and in its ambiguity, often misleading.

Neither society as a group, nor its institutions or laws, can define ethics or regulate ethical or moral behavior. It can only deal with unethical behavior when that behavior is congruent with illegal activity. The law must settle for that. Ethics cannot. The law in its position of institutional power may lose sight of the fact that relationships exist in more than one plane. Institutional relationships do not require a personal bond. Vital (personal) relationships do, but law cannot effectively regulate those relationships. So long as we remain a group, our laws will not—cannot—be entirely ethical in spite of what society claims.

To move beyond the basic—vital—relationships of being and becoming to the larger, active perspective of living in the world, we'll have to deal with the reality of living in the societal milieu. A workable plan—a system of principles for guidance in practical affairs would be helpful. Let's start by developing a philosophy for accomplishing just that.

CHAPTER THREE

Developing A Philosophy For Living

*A philosophy is nothing more than a set of
principles for guidance in practical affairs.*

Permanent solutions to mankind's problems are realized only in the context of life—the individual or humanity—not the group. If we hope to solve the problems of life and living, we must work in the context of vital entities–humanity, community and ourselves–and not rely on institutions and groups. It's up to you.

Philosophy Defined

Philosophy's celebrated rhetoric, speculation and popular tendency to be judged by scientific standards have effectively damned it to a forgotten corner of academia. Too bad. We need philosophy because science as we know it can't answer the vital questions we have to deal with. Philosophy can.

The essential mission of philosophy is the search for a secure basis for human happiness—*the good life.* The practice of philosophy has been defined as a means of thinking rationally and critically about fundamental questions of life; however, "thinking rationally" risks thinking scientifically. Science has effectively appropriated the concept of logical thinking into what's been immortalized as "the scientific method," limiting itself by requiring that everything be proven before being fully accepted. The fact that philosophy knows no such limits is its major strength, not a weakness. Givens do not have to be justified.

Ethics is that very practical element of philosophy dealing with moral principles. The system of principles that we'll deal with here involves First Principles (think: givens) and the very practical matter of living the good life.

In order to apply philosophy to living, there really are only two questions we need to answer:

1. What is it (what does it mean), and
2. What do I have to do to achieve it?

Who's kidding who? Are we so presumptuous as to believe that we can really answer the question that seems to have baffled mankind since well before Year One: *What Is the Meaning of Life?* Well, why not?

And if we forgo the semantic games for which philosophy is *in*famous, we can not only answer that question with regard to the project at hand, but we can go well beyond that. And we shall.

Cutting somewhat prematurely to the chase, just what *is* the meaning of life? Try this for starters:

The meaning of life is living.

Too simple? Allow me to define living in the current context. The ABCs of living can be stated:

- **A**cknowledging (yourself, others as individuals, humanity, and *what is*);
- **B**ecoming (who you are);
- **C**reating (bridging the gap between becoming and…)
- Contributing (to both society and humanity.)

A has been immortalized, if incompletely, by Descartes:

"I think; therefore I am"

Among other things, thinking verifies both the individual and his intellect, linking the physical individual with his conceptual mind. But thinking is abstract. Nothing happens without doing and, since connection and progression are inevitable, living-doing inevitably follows life-being. We might expand on Descartes with:

I become, therefore I am

This at least gets us to the point of the unique individual, but that's not enough. Doing is applied being. The fact that you *are* counts only if you fully commit to all that it implies. To develop a philosophy for living, we'll have to move beyond being. So, to give Descartes' assertion a shot of life, we might say "I act on my thoughts, therefore I am" or, more simply:

I do, therefore I am.

Thinking is abstract and personal, living is not. It is accomplished within the context of the whole of humanity. Without humanity we have neither being nor meaning. It is in humanity that we are created and become, exist and progress. Humanity is where what we think, feel and do, takes form.

Remember, who you are is what you **do** with what you are. While what you are is beyond your control, what you do is a function of your unique self. You alone are totally accountable for what you do, making you responsible as well for who you are because you are the only one who will do what you will do as you can do it. And when you take this step, you enter the realm of creativity.

In order to articulate the meaning of life, there's no avoiding the phenomenon of creating, because that's what we do. Constantly. If the meaning of life is living, life's *purpose* is creating. And we each create in our own unique way.

You can't help but create. The very act of living your unique life is creative. Nobody's ever lived your life before. You process everything uniquely, different from the way anyone else ever did, does or ever will. That's *creative*. Because you are unique, your every conscious action is unique and creative. Read this again.

We've already covered the basics of responsible creating: begin with the truth (your honesty validates your self); deal with others as you would be dealt with; do no harm; trust in the givens; and accept responsibility for yourself.

So the meaning of life comes down to this: acknowledging, becoming, doing, contributing and creating, *responsibly*. It's what to do. It comes down to living—morally resolving relationships between our *selfs* and the rest of humanity.

So, put succinctly, finally, and even reversibly:

I CREATE, THEREFORE I AM.

Think for a moment on the awesome power of that simple assertion. Now you really **are**. This, the true meaning of life, the Power to Create, is your power. What more could you ask?

Assuming that you want the good life, to live it you'll have to make the right choices.

Making the Right Choices - Ethics

The fact that you *are* is a given. You didn't choose to be, but here you are. So it is with truth. You don't choose truth. It comes with being—a vital, universal principle and an integral part of humanity and your connection with it. You can ignore it (many do) but it never goes away.

Ethical concepts and legal concepts are often confused with one another, but they're not alike. Manmade standards are embodied in customs and the law. They may be collective, but they're not universal. Laws are often imperfect and subject to opinion—they can be changed. Ethics can't. Ethics is not subject to opinion. It answers only to truth. Ethics is universal; it is before the law and does not require the law. The law may or may not spring from ethics. All too often it does not.

While it is considered to be a difficult subject, when approached head-on ethics can become quite simple (maybe not easy, but simple). For now we'll use the terms ethics and morality interchangeably. While not academically rigorous, doing so will at least allow us to treat the subject in a straightforward manner while avoiding becoming mired in semantics. Later we'll make a distinction.

Difficulties in dealing with ethics and morality begin when we fail to see (or choose to avoid) their inherent truth. Morality is about virtue, integrity, character, and similar verities (another word for givens), and words like these can make us uneasy. We tend to become uncertain when confronting absolutes like perfection. (In fact, this uncertainty is the reason why many of us deny the very idea of absolutes like perfection and avoid the truth of ethics.) It's difficult to approach the idea of perfection with confidence, but that's exactly what must be done to get to the heart of the matter. Just because we can't *be* perfect doesn't mean we can't appreciate the concept. Besides, it's easy.

Being ethical can be thought of simply as right being. Being, in this context, means existence and authenticity, which in turn mean truth. Right means correct, valid, accurate, precise, genuine; not "right" by my definition, nor the court's, nor any put forth by any institution or group no matter how learned. Ethics and morality do not require confirmation by anyone for verification. They are whole and positive in and of themselves, easier to know than to define.

Doubts? Well, look at it this way:

Do the following qualities have any negative aspects? Are they ever really wrong in the long run?

virtue	goodness	purity
integrity	compassion	empathy
excellence	decency	honesty
courtesy	respect	patience
dignity	character	forgiveness
honor	tolerance	understanding

Are there laws that protect us from any of these qualities? Why not? Because they are universally understood as qualities that can only benefit us and mankind.

But as we all know, this isn't a perfect world. These simple concepts have been clouded by what we perceive as reality. We are removed from them by what we perceive to be facts of life (but are better described as facts of living). In this context we've invented *situation ethics*, a convenient play on words implying that ethics is relative to the situation. But circumstances cannot change ethical principles. They are inviolate.

To close this loop, let's take a look at the other side of the coin:

corruption	hatred	wickedness
insolence	impertinence	enmity
vice	intolerance	contempt
arrogance	fraud	disrespect
scorn	depravity	hostility
degeneracy	debauchery	obscenity

Are any of these qualities admirable, advocated as a way of life? In fact, there are laws protecting us from many of them. Why? Because they are universally known to be inherently destructive, to have no redeeming qualities. They are, in fact, immoral.

As an integral part of mankind, all of us have the necessary ethical parts without any action, or even presence, of another—one can be ethical alone. It does not require sanction. It simply (but maybe not so easily) requires right being, and that's not a simple matter because of pressures put on us by countless others who would have us be otherwise. But it's not required to act as others would have us act; we can choose to do so or not. The decision to act is individual, and so is the accountability. Each of us is, in the final analysis, responsible for ourselves and accountable to mankind, and our actions ought to reflect this.

What we're really talking about here is autonomy. Autonomy presupposes humanity and the mutual dependence necessary for its survival. We are entitled to be ourselves. Our autonomy is a right–a given—and innately ethical.

Ethics – The System of *Universal Moral Principle*

Ethics has its roots in First Principles, the foremost being absolute truth—perfection. The frustration of coming up with a good definition using standard references increases in proportion to their number. It is immediately apparent that the first hurdle is the written word.

A branch of philosophy... can bring us to a full stop, never mind the ambiguity of *the study of the nature of morals*(?) *and of specific moral choices...* (whatever they may be). *Rules of conduct* fails, because anyone could define his own rules of conduct according to his own standards, all of which would be "ethical" by this definition. If this were true, then ethical would not be the wholly positive term that we intuitively know it to be.

While ethics may indeed be an area of study and a branch of philosophy, neither of these definitions helps at all when trying to explain what ethics means in the sense of being ethical, universally understood as a wholly positive state of being. Being unethical is universally understood as negative.

*We need a universally applicable definition of ethics that supports its adjective **ethical.*** Ethics is not the plural of ethic (both are singular). An ethic is a body of values governing a particular group (the operative words here are *group* and *values*). Suffice to say that values (and any ethic that may be connected with them) are set by the group and cannot be extrapolated beyond the group. Neither the group nor its values are necessarily universal. But as an integral part of humanity, ethics (the one with an *s*) is universal–vital and inviolate. Ethics is, in fact, the standard by which any ethic is measured. Ethics is not right, true or good as defined by anyone. Ethics is universally right as opposed to wrong, universally good as opposed to bad, universally true as opposed to false. It is right being. That which is ethical is right. That which is ethical is good. That which is ethical is true.

Conversely, that which is wrong can only be unethical. That which is bad can only be unethical. That which is false can only be unethical.

Ethics is central to our intellect–everyone *knows* it–and can only be understood in terms of that intellect. Ethics can be studied, debated, explained and disputed, certainly misunderstood, but ethics cannot be changed.

While right and good may be open to debate, truth is not. And stripped to its bare bones, the root of ethics is Truth with a capital T. And, in its only context (humanity), ethics can be defined as

The System of Universal Moral Principle.

Perfect? Hardly. But if ethics is difficult to define, consider its source— truth. It's a fact that one cannot prove a principle using that which the principle begets. For example, philosophy cannot be defined using science, itself a child of philosophy. Therein lies the difficulty in defining truth using words which we have invented to define our ideas. Because truth is perfect— a timeless given—a First Principle. It is, in fact, *the* First Principle. Everything that *is* springs from it. First principles are those ideas that every rational being can't *not* know. They are inborn to us just like our minds, an essential part of what makes us human. To claim that we do not know them is not open to question; it is instead moral denial. Want proof? Try *Conscience.* Every rational human being has one.

So philosophy (the pursuit of truth), being derivative of truth, cannot be used to prove its parent. However, we need a definition that satisfies our idea of the concept in order to proceed—after all, that's what words are for. Allow me to posit a definition (not original) of truth based on perfection: *a verified or indisput-*

able fact, proposition, principle; being in accord with reality; in other words, **what is**. This admittedly imperfect definition will be used here and henceforth.

Ethics/truth is consistent across time. What was ethical/true then is ethical/true now and will be ethical/true in the future, but without some sort of application, ethics would be an empty formal abstraction to be studied, debated, explained and disputed, even misunderstood (but not changed!). In fact, ethics has suffered study, debate and dispute by countless others and in the process, has become an empty formal abstraction. It's time to return to the basics. In doing so we'll distinguish between ethics and morality so that we can move beyond the individual.

The M Words

While the words may look and even sound alike, there are significant differences in meaning between moral, morals and morality (and we can throw in mores for good measure). Morals and mores are both nouns with their roots firmly planted in society; they are described in cultural terms. Moral, the singular noun, is an ambiguous term that can mean anything from lesson to platitude to principle (but it cannot be used to redefine principle because it is derivative of it). Morality and its adjective, moral, are concepts founded in that old absolute, truth. (If this were not so, morality would have no basis at all.)

From here on, morality will be used in the context of ethical (honest) conduct—doing. Morality will be considered as applied ethics; therefore, if the essence of ethics is truth, then

$$\text{Morality} = \text{applied truth} = \text{HONESTY}$$
in the context of humanity.

If ethics defines right being, then morality (and moral, the adjective) defines right doing. So the roots of ethics and morality can be reduced to absolute truth and honesty. Morality is, like ethics, an integral element of mankind, not a product of it. It's universal. There are no man-made standards for ethical or moral conduct. They simply are. They are absolute. They are known and, whether or not you realize it, you know them. You only have to employ them.

Applied Ethics and Community

In the spirit of presenting basic concepts in a simple way, we've distinguished between the individual, the group and humanity to emphasize important differences between vital (living) entities and others. Family and community weren't discussed beyond correctly defining their primary importance to the continuance of mankind.

The earlier discussion of groups was important to illustrate the distinction between vital and non-vital entities. Groups, which include political, social and religious organizations, institutions such as government and schools, clubs and other aggregations of individuals brought together to get things done, may be useful and even inevitable, but they're not vital to humanity.

True community is not a group. Remember that a group is formed to get something done, to satisfy a particular need. Communities are not formed so much as they become, forming themselves to satisfy vital needs. True community is a vital and ethical entity (and, not insignificantly, usually short on laws).

The phenomenon of connection discussed earlier is the basis and substance of community. In fact, the mutual vitality created by the personal connection of two individuals (discussed earlier) is a principle of community. Another is interdependence, and still another is responsibility. While the major distinction between the community and the group is the presence or absence of a vital connection, there are parallels, not the least of which is that neither can dictate beyond itself. However, the vital connection necessary for community implies that any rules set by a community be in accord with moral principle. True community is fundamentally ethical, whereas the group need not be.

Although each individual in the community may not be linked directly with each other member, there is that same common vital thread—interdependence—that links members of a family, the same thread that links the past with the future. Without that thread there is no continuity and therefore no life. Without it there is only a group.

A number of positive qualities were introduced in the discussion of ethics:

virtue	goodness	purity
integrity	compassion	empathy
excellence	decency	honesty
courtesy	respect	patience
dignity	character	forgiveness
honor	tolerance	understanding

It's not accidental that all these words and others like them describe characteristics found in true community. They encourage the free exchange of ideas, betterment and growth–becoming–characteristic of community. Community grows—becomes–by the power of the multiple combined strengths of the various individuals comprising it, not on the basis of getting something done.

Morality is really the "operating system" of humanity. Just as being ethical requires truth, morality requires dealing honestly with others. Honesty applies truth beyond the individual. Not to be redundant, but to be perfectly clear, honesty is the linchpin of morality. And the key to the good life lies in moral–honest and responsible–relationships.

Our morality begins in the milieu in which we become: family and community. This is where we make the transition from human *being* to human doing. Learning begins here on a foundation of ethics and morality. Family and community automatically provide ethical access to humanity and all its collective knowledge. Remember, family and community are not groups. They are reciprocally personal relationships based on vital bonds like blood, ethnicity, and heritage. They define and direct initially who we are. A common and vital morality connects members of community and family to the past and the future. Without that connection there's no vitality, no continuity. Without that connection there is only a group.

Groups are of us but they neither define nor direct us. In fact, individuals like you define and direct them. Institutions, governments, religions, even whole societies, only exist to get something done. When it's done, so is the reason for the group. Those differences between groups and living entities point toward those differences between relationships that must be understood. Virtually every one of society's problems can be traced to problems in relationships, and living is all about relationships.

Shared relationships (such as those in family and community) involve commitment of both parties; these have a life of their own. Such relationships survive, grow and work because: 1) they are founded in ethics and trust; 2) they involve morality; and 3) they require responsibility.

Moral living means doing, thinking, acting, relating honestly in the context of humanity. And living the good life requires that we relate morally– honestly–with our fellow man.

The individual has no limits, remember? Connection is inevitable and progression is inescapable, just as night follows day. Time does not stop. We may as well go with the flow because it flows in spite of us. If we do (and no matter *what* we do), more will be created, and we are integral to that creation.

So There you have it: ***Ethics Unwrapped***.

Unpacked and opened for use. Try it. You'll like it.

Now that we've settled the meaning of life, we can put the second question *What do I do here and now (anywhere, any time)?* to rest as well:

You initiate, cause, develop, invent, produce, make, generate, beget, achieve, accomplish, devise, build, construct. You endeavor to bring about what will extend, stretch or expand your (and therefore humanity's) envelope. You continue to become. You *create*. And in doing so honestly and responsibly, you further the progress of humanity. The Power of One! *Your* power!

But don't forget the other side of the coin–what responsibility!

Because we have responsibility, we're obliged to be honest about it. As a card-carrying member of humanity, it's your responsibility to be moral. It is, in fact, your only responsibility. Your responsibility to humanity is to be ethical and to act morally. That's all you have to do, anywhere and anytime, under all circumstances.

So the answer to the second question, what to do right here and right now, is the same as the first: Become and create, responsibly, and resolve relationships between yourself and the rest of humanity morally.

Thus our philosophy is essentially complete. Let's see how it can be employed to save humanity from itself...

CHAPTER FOUR

Beyond Community

B ecause every relationship is unique, each of us is responsible for our own. And because relationships involve more than one individual, communication is necessary.

While perfect communication is virtually impossible, that founded in truth– honesty–stands the best chance of success over the long run. Principled (honest) behavior is, in fact, crucial to humanity. And we know it when we see it, whether or not we acknowledge it, just as most rational beings intuitively know when "something's wrong."

Unfortunately, it seems to be human nature to want to either rely on others excessively or disregard them entirely. You can choose to do neither because neither course works beyond the short run. Instead, choose to appreciate yourself for who you really are and consider others similarly, and you will enjoy personal freedom, peace and serenity, and be on course for the good life.

Begin with the givens, the constants, those things that you can count on that will be there even if you aren't: time, light, gravity, the earth, sun and moon, life itself. Begin at black and white, not gray. The givens are real and they are free: you, your own existence, individuality and uniqueness, as well as your brain, mind, imagination and intuition, not to mention your articulated body with its automatic breathing and heartbeat. Just accept them and use them. Responsibly.

Your connection with humanity, that thread connecting each of us with the past and to the future, is valid, and progression is inevitable. These are more truths that you can count on, so use them freely.

You have the capacity to choose to do this at any time, alone, without anyone else's permission. Simply choose to be honest with yourself. Then,

choose to communicate honestly and base your relationships on honesty. Only you can do this.

It should be clear at this point that the unique individual (you) is the major driving force for mankind, that overarching natural system of which we are an integral part; and that each individual is, literally, one-of-a-kind, linked by our own unique mind to that positive vital principle that formed him and all of humanity on its terms, not ours. Truth is the seed of being. To start with less is an exercise in futility. It's a given, and so are you, so accept the gifts and find the answers.

In fact, nothing could be simpler, more effective or more valid. Truth is the principal principle for living right. In order to extend ethical behavior beyond yourself to relationships, merely add three words from Hippocrates: *Do no harm.*

This, in fact, is basic morality. Live it and be fulfilled as a human being. You need only make the choice to do so. Actually doing it is effortless. Amazing, isn't it? Once you've made the choice, it's done!

*Acknowledge, accept, appreciate, affirm and apply what **is** (the givens–all of them); and support others in doing the same.* It's simple. It's painless. What's stopping you?

Well, you might think at this point that something's missing, and you might be right. So far we've dealt with the ideal what-to-do. Honest relationships between the individual and humanity may be all that are required, but they're not all that exist. And the elsewhere in which they do exist is where the problems lie. That elsewhere is the group.

The Individual's Relationship With The Group

A person relates differently to the group than he does with individuals in the group, because the group is a *what*, while the individual is a *who*. This profound difference needs to be appreciated if we are to understand why the individual relates to groups in a different way than he relates to humanity (made up exclusively of *whos*) in general.

From the point of view of the individual, a favorable relationship with a group will satisfy his need(s) without causing him to lose a significant part of his personal value. And, because he is vital and the group is not, the individual–not the group–is responsible for his group relationships.

Any individual may quit any group at any time with no change in his standing as a human being and no damage to his human dignity. Any real loss is the group's because it loses some portion of its assumed vitality. The power of the individual. Something to keep in mind…

The Group's Relationship With The Individual

From the standpoint of the group, a favorable relationship is one with individuals having similar interests or needs, and the desire to help meet group goals. The group serves individuals by providing support, protection, stimulation and/or consensus, and/or to serve humanity by augmenting the effects of individuals. A sustainable group will improve conditions for both itself and the individual. Remember, the group exists to **serve**, not exploit, the individual and/or mankind. If it opposes any of the basic precepts of humanity, it acts in opposition to basic verities. Any group that assumes omnipotence oversteps its bounds and is doomed to eventual failure.

While a group can help stimulate individual growth, there may be a real cost to the individual. Any group extracts some amount of freedom from its members in exchange for group identification, but the group does not have the power to change the individual without his consent. It may reject anyone for its own reasons, making it appear that the individual is at its mercy; however, no group has real power over anyone without his consent; and remember this: *the individual always retains the prerogative to choose or reject a group without risking his dignity as an individual.*

Group Relationships as a Source Of Conflict

Problems develop when the individual/group relationship is misunderstood, misrepresented or abused. The group, being larger and more visible, may appear more powerful. It may appropriate greater authority and its members may assume greater importance than "outsiders," forgetting that it's the individual who really makes the choices.

A group with an exaggerated idea of its own importance may equate itself with community or even claim to speak for mankind (think churches or society). This—placing the institution above the individual—discriminates against or even subverts humanity. But in the last analysis, any group is at the mercy of any individual. The significance of this statement cannot be over-emphasized.

None of the foregoing says that conflict has to be an essential by-product of the group. Groups often are instruments of good. It is only when they fail to honor the individual or humanity that they cease to be agents for progress.

The foregoing discussion illustrates the differences between group relationships and vital ones, and how those relationships operate with differing effects upon humanity. What's happened is that group relationships have overtaken vital ones and, in the process, changed our very perception of relationships themselves. This process has been detrimental to humanity and has resulted in the current situation. To describe how this has happened we'll have to return once again to the beginning. But before you do so, read this paragraph again.

CHAPTER FIVE

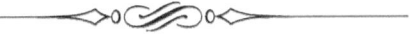

Resolution Of The Problem

We've seen how the system developed and how it has overtaken us. The progression seems reasonable to a fault, yet the results are certainly less than perfect. Why?

The rapid growth of knowledge and technology encouraged sharing the load of developing, harvesting, employing and enjoying its fruits. It had to be this way—there's simply too much for any one person, family and/or community to know or deal with. Besides, we're not all interested in (or good at) the same things.

There's nothing inherently wrong with group involvement in the advance of humanity. To cover everything that must be dealt with, we share the load, and we do it rather well. Each of us tends to specialize in what interests us most, and we each go about it in our own way, just a little differently from the way someone else might do it. We also share responsibility. That we do this at all illustrates the innate wholeness of mankind, and that we do it as well as we do speaks volumes for the innate goodness of mankind. While each of us can make an individual contribution, groups can increase our effectiveness manifold and enable us to progress collectively as far as we care to go. In the process, each of us has access to all the resources of mankind at any time. What's wrong with that? Nothing.

It is, in fact, the way things really are *if* we do it right. Apparently we haven't. Let's focus on what went wrong and why by returning yet again to square one.

Our first contacts beyond the family exposed each of us to societal morals (which, importantly, are different from morality). The influence of societal morals on each one of us has been profound and various, and not always positive.

Once an individual achieves some degree of independence in the family environment, he takes his experiences, for better or for worse, with him into the community, and from there into the world at large (and its groups). He also takes with him certain rights which he must guard with his life.

Rights

Remember those givens we continue to mention? Well, those universal truths number among our rights. They're ours simply by virtue of our being. They need not and cannot be bestowed on us because we already own them.

In addition to open access to sunlight, air, gravity and the natural phenomena available to us all, we own the right to be (and to become). We own the right to use our own senses and motor skills (within ethical limits), the right to make choices, the right to protect ourselves, the right to employ our own intellect and the right to be the unique and private individuals that we are. But these rights (and others), being universal, are equivalent. While you own yours, so does everyone else own theirs, so you may not infringe on their rights which, being universal, are the same as—equal to—yours.

Those rights include as well certain responsibilities—obligations—which are nothing more than the other side of the same coin—rights from the perspective of humankind. *Our obligations are just as much a birthright as the rights we covet.*

You also have the right to create, to advocate for humanity, to accept full responsibility for the consequences of your choices and actions, and to permit others to do the same. That's ethics—just the way it is. No group can cause it to be otherwise. Givens are givens, like it or not. These responsibilities are as much yours as your breathing and your heartbeat, whether or not you choose to accept them, and neither you nor any group has the power to change that or refer them to other groups. Everyone has them.

By discharging those rights (and obligations) morally, we would automatically enable and expand the free society that we all seek. Humanity is an entity that lives despite any one of us–an example of *spontaneous order*. The world is, after all, an ethical whole from which it is impossible to entirely banish morality. No government or its laws can prevail against it in the long run.

But we haven't satisfied our part of the bargain. And by not doing so—by not exercising our rights and discharging our obligations—we have effectively abdicated to society (a group) our rights in exchange for mere privileges.

Privileges

We've noted that in writing its laws, society necessarily employs definitions appropriate to its aims. Just as with equality, it has in fact done exactly that with the word rights. The law tells us that we have, for instance, "the right to remain silent. "But it can't. We already own that right (to speak or not to speak is a matter of individual choice) and certain others as well, independent of society and before its law. Our rights as human beings are absolute—*givens*. What society's law bestows are more properly privileges. Privileges, like any group rules, may be changed, deleted, or added at the pleasure of the group. But when society tampers with our rights (or definitions thereof) either deliberately or accidentally, it risks fouling the system. And that's what's happened.

Privileges include the freedom to pass relatively unhampered through and about our society while enjoying our rights in the group context, and abiding by and benefiting from group rules. We also ostensibly have the privilege of freely speaking our minds. Many societies (and some groups within our own) do not bestow that privilege.

The confusion of privileges with rights is a function of a widespread misunderstanding of the relationship between ethics and values.

Values

Values, like privileges but unlike ethics, are not absolute. They may be defined by a group or society itself, or they may be defined by an individual. But whatever they may or may not be, values, like morals, are not universal.

Values are relative, defined ideals, customs, mores and morals. Values may be described, delimited, designated or interpreted by an individual, community or society. They may be either positive or negative. Ethics, on the other hand, can only be positive.

To put the difference between ethics and values in perspective, recall the difference between morality (honesty) and morals (that in spite of being generally-accepted societal customs, need not always be strictly moral), and consider the sociological aspects of everyday living in a society dominated by groups.

If a society's values are not universal, the ethical individual may have difficulty trying to deal with them. But society does not persuade us to be perfect, only to "go along to get along" for the good of the many. (In fact, society and its laws persuade us to be *alike*, not unique, because it is easier to deal with, and regulate, similar entities.) It is within this framework that society's rules and laws are written: just accept society's values and obey its laws, and everyone will get along. If only...

Group Privileges, Values and Rules

All that being said, it remains that any society needs a system of rules within which its members can operate to the general benefit. These rules are founded in its values and articulated in its privileges and laws. But while the rules of all successful societies including our own may begin in ethics and are adapted to the society's needs and wishes, it's in the adaptation that ethics often suffers.

Our own rules trace their origin to a paramount need for freedom. Our own positive law began with a Declaration of Independence from our mother country empowered by a Constitution written by individuals with a strong ethical and moral base "in order to form a more perfect union."

Drawing upon the experience of past cultures and societies in order to weave the strongest, most equitable and serviceable fabric possible at the time, a document creating a republic representing the best the world had to offer was codified in a few short pages by an unusual group of dedicated individuals. (You may wish to point out that this was a group, and that I have come down hard on groups. I would maintain, however, that this group got it pretty much right, and concur that groups are capable of doing good.) Its first ten amendments spelled out what the government was *not* empowered to do with regard to its citizens. The Bill Of Rights clearly maintains the primacy of the individual. While not perfect (it was known not to be, hence the modifier more to the absolute perfect), it was a job well done that has served us admirably.

It may be of interest to note at this point that "these truths that we hold to be self-evident": life, liberty and the pursuit of happiness, are precisely that—truths, givens, underpinnings of morality.

Even the law of our own society, arguably a high-water mark of the world's civilizations, does not apply globally. Other societies and cultures are free to exist and govern as they please. Enlightened as it may be, our society cannot intrude on others at its option. It is a group, after all. Nor is it empowered to go beyond its own limits, even within itself.

The point is that any group—our society included—has limits even within itself beyond which it may not dictate what its members may or may not do. Ethics—truth—is one of these. No group, however well-intended, may tamper with truth or define it in any way other than the absolute. Furthermore, while our society may pass laws that ignore or disregard truth even if these laws would benefit that group, those laws cannot stand within the whole of mankind, and therefore cannot apply to mankind or its members across-the-board. And no matter how many groups we belong to or how varied they are, each of us is a member of humanity first, and First Principles trump all others.

The conflict can only be resolved by the individual, who stands at the very center of it. In fact, *you* control it by virtue of your humanity and innate ethics. Any society or government is limited in its powers by its own laws, and no society or government may ethically exceed these powers regardless of its wishes. Neither society nor its governments can prevail against mankind or the ethical individual.

The individual has certain powers by virtue of his humanity, not to mention those granted by law. When there is a conflict, the individual must look beyond his privileges (granted by the group) to his rights (granted by his very being), and he is not only empowered but obligated to resolve the conflict in the interest of mankind. If the conflict involves ethics, there is no contest. Ethics is the only choice.

Resolving Problems With Group Relationships

Society's worst problems occur in the context of the group because society is a group. These problems tend to affect more people to a greater degree than would a conflict between individuals. Relationships within or between groups are in fact the source of major societal problems (think war).

It's inevitable that individuals will connect and groups will form. The combinations of individuals and groups are endless, and their relationships complex. If relationships are complex, it follows that problems with relationships must be complex as well.

But complex problems don't have to have complex solutions. Always simplify. Start by reducing previous discussions to the basics (not in any particular rank or order):

- Of the three basic entities, only the individual and humanity are vital and permanent. Groups are transient, subject to societal change.
- Groups are instruments for getting things done, not always the same as doing.
- Groups may make their own laws that do not apply beyond themselves.
- Groups serve individuals and humanity—it's not the other way around.

It's essential to regard individuals separately from the groups they form, and the group apart from the whole of humankind.

The group has no power over the individual without his consent; the group's connection with the individual can be severed without threatening the vitality of the individual (not only true, but a source of considerable individual power).

Any legitimate solution to any problem, including those dealing with relationships, must be able to stand the test of time. A permanent solution can be realized only in the context of life—the individual or humanity—not the group.

Most problems with groups are caused by conflict between group rules and individual rights, needs, desires and beliefs. Using group rules to resolve problems with individual relationships may not be successful. An individual in conflict with the group may try to resolve differences between them, but if the differences can't be resolved, the solution may require his leaving the group.

While the group may be part of the problem, it may not be part of the solution. In the extreme case, *any* group can be sacrificed with no permanent danger to either the individual or humanity.

Speaking of extreme cases, the group always faces the peril of extinction because its power is not intrinsic. Group power is provided by or taken from the individual. But even if the group ceases to be, nothing vital is at risk. Individual and humanity not only remain intact, they continue to move forward. This is an important truth to keep in mind.

The individual is the defining element; he has vitality, knowledge, and power. He can relate to any other individual, and he can and should maintain his *self* while being part of a group.

Problems with relationships must be solved by the individual.

The Individual Connection

We have demonstrated how development of the group has insidiously overpowered the individual-humankind relationship, becoming the tail that now wags the dog, but how are we to get around the problem? After all, no one of us can hope to relate personally to billions of individuals speaking hundreds of languages and dialects, and there are so many groups available with which to associate that it seems quite natural to identify with the few that seem to fit our needs. In fact, we seem to be compelled by what we believe to be our individual limitations to deal directly with only a small fraction of humanity, and groups seem to provide the answer.

The fact that these relationships have failed to deliver the good life, however, requires that we back up and look at the situation from the individual's point of view. We have to retrace our steps from the point of view of the individual and his development so that we can find where we erred and how we, individually, can correct the situation.

Blaming society is futile because, as we've demonstrated, the group is incapable of fundamentally correcting the situation. It's the individual who has to shoulder the greater part of the load. Rather than rely on the group, any group, we have to think and do for ourselves. We are and always were free to make choices. We have to retrace our steps and see where we made the wrong ones.

Actually, we've already retraced our steps here to some degree in the process of identifying the group dilemma. One simplistic but effective solution that follows is to simply choose to take back our relationships outside of the group. This doesn't mean abandoning groups, it requires only that we recognize groups for what they are and maintain our vital relationships outside of them. This has to work, because any one of us is more than half of any relationship.

Each one of us is free to do so at any time. To actually do it, however, requires a basic change in approach. How to accomplish this change has been discussed earlier, but now we'll look at it again from a different perspective: that of the mature/whole individual not encumbered by group think.

Maturity And Interdependence

Our world is a truly wonderful place, no less so because of thousands of years of human development and use (and yes, abuse) of it. There's more to see, taste, feel, smell, hear and do than time to experience even a small part of it. And this progress multiplies with every year that we occupy it.

There are those who believe that we're on the verge of knowing it all. After all, how much further can we go, especially since the pace is increasing so quickly? It seems like at this rate all the answers are almost within our grasp, *if only...*

Maybe yes, probably no, but that's not the point. What *is* the point is that, at this stage of our development, we're caught up in (and limited by) a scientific approach to a world dominated by our five senses. If we hope to ever know it all, we will have to change our approach drastically. In what ways, and how, is what we're about to explore in more detail.

We know that we're born totally dependent and that we can't survive without others. But from birth we start on the road to independence, using everything and everyone available to us. That we almost immediately disregard our inherent dependency as we move beyond it testifies to our aptitude for ignoring the basics.

The drive of individuals toward independence is a natural product of recognizing their uniqueness. It's perfectly natural for the developing individual to seek independence, and, most importantly it is only after achieving some measure of it that they learn the important difference between being independent and being not dependent.

The individual's move toward independence is encouraged by others because it is in mankind's best interest that we not be dependent. Humanity knows that the drive toward individual independence is that same vitality which makes progress inevitable. However, this inevitability can overshadow its origins and cause us to ignore the fact that *none of it could have happened without others.* More importantly, it also overshadows its future by insinuating that, being independent, one can go it alone.

It's true that after some point, an individual might be able to survive alone, but without some connection to some other at some time, his life will have little meaning. We know that any relationship becomes greater than its parts (1+1>2). Without this synergy–this creation of more from less that drives humanity forward–there can be no progress.

So perfect independence is impossible. Just as it's impossible to spontaneously create oneself, just as it's impossible to become without others, so is it impossible to be without others. None of us were ever, and cannot ever be, totally independent and still maintain our vital connection. But we can become *not* dependent. Mature individuals are *interdependent*.

Interdependence means a mutual reliance, not necessarily direct but acknowledged just the same. All individuals are mutually dependent by way of their common relationship—that vital thread—with humanity, the realm in which every one of us functions. Human interdependence is another given. And, like any given, ignoring, forgetting or denying it doesn't negate it.

The chronically dependent—immature—individual may have a temporary negative effect on humanity, but that will pass. However, the rare person achieving total independence has a permanent negative effect (and is, thereby, immoral). Total independence acts to destroy humanity itself by severing that vital link giving meaning to life. Of course, humanity will survive, even advance, in spite of what any individual does because it will outlast him, but it works better when all its parts function as a whole - when each of us is a vital part of the whole of humanity.

Mature individuals accept both their humanity and their interdependence. They know that they can neither fulfill nor be fulfilled without others. They know that with synergy, individuals can enjoy much more than they would by pursuing their own selfish ends. But even mature individuals may lose sight of what's important. They may become group oriented rather than maintain an overall concern for humanity (and it's in the nature of the group to perpetuate this tendency). They may concentrate on getting something done at the expense of being and becoming.

As we grow, we develop our senses, enjoy the fruits of our labors, and savor the lack of dependence we foster both in ourselves and others, but as we join groups that have similar interests, we may forget our dependencies. Accepting them and all givens unconditionally is as it should be, but in doing so we should not forget them. Not acknowledging our givens—ignoring the basics—is one reason we're in our present situation.

The sooner we accept and acknowledge the givens—all of them including the fact that we have limited control over the consequences of our actions— the sooner we will truly mature and come to be what we could be.

While becoming and progress are virtually ensured, maturity is not. That is developed individually. Just because we survive and develop does not guarantee that we will mature. Maturity requires a working brain and a degree of conscious individual input. Should this input be replaced by group activity, maturity may be slow in coming and may never actually occur. This major problem has to be recognized before it can be overcome.

We've spent considerable time pointing out problems with and of group relationships that must be understood if they are to be solved. A major problem that we've isolated is this:

In the heat of progress, group relationships have displaced individual relationships.

As group problems proliferate, it becomes more and more difficult to see the trees for the forest and overcome the inertia resulting from and 'larger groups. It doesn't help that society multiplies the problem by planting more trees.

Humanity, the universe within which the issue resides and within which it must be resolved, is where the answers lie, and you, an integral element of humanity, are the source of those answers.

Family, the locus of moral teaching and focus of moral action, is the elemental vital relationship, the basic medium by which each of us enters the world. As a given, it does not go away. Family defines each of us for better or worse and has a significant effect on our earliest connections beyond it. We tend to associate with those with whom we are comfortable and have a vital relationship. This wholly positive phenomenon is strongly associated with our very survival.

But life transcends family. Individuals tend to move naturally from family into community and as they do, tend to keep their connections intact. While community is not a group, there are similarities. For instance, both influence the individuals comprising them. Both benefit from shared efforts, neither can dictate effectively beyond itself.

It's the differences that are critical. Community as a moral establishment is built on the reciprocally vital relationship of individuals who, left to their own devices, tend to live by sensibility, intuition and emotion rather than by the rule of law. The rule of law may be necessary in the group environment, but not in community. Why? Because community is not a group. It is an ethical microcosm of humanity. Community nurtures, protects and respects its progeny, investing in them and relying on them to carry on not only as individuals, but as part of the community. In community they learn not only how to do things but what to avoid, and more importantly, to be and become themselves. This vital dimension is missing from many groups.

The major difference between community and the group is the ethical connection. True community is built on a reciprocally personal relationship based on a vital bond related to the person rather than the institution. Community is defined by ethics, not by any group or its laws.

The Individual - Key To All Relationships

While family and community provide the individual with a vital link with humanity, the individual is key to it all. While humanity is the source, the reservoir and the lifeline, the individual is the elemental and definitive component. Individuals can relate to any other individual on an equal basis; they need not be limited by any group to which they may belong. Within the context of humanity they have no limits, and because individuals represent more than half of any relationship, they have power beyond themselves. *They can create change.*

All well and good, you say. Now we know what the problem is, even how it came to be, and theoretically how to solve it. But this is the real world we're talking about, and you're telling me that one person can change it?

YES!

It only takes one person to change the world, and any one of us, including you, can be that person. It's been done before (Consider Alexander the Great or any number of historical figures who have done just that).[1]

This is admittedly a lot to swallow. But let's look at the situation from another angle, the standpoint of the individual's—*your*—place in the global context.

The individual has immediate access via humankind to the resources to not only figure out what's wrong, but to change what's wrong, and the ethical right (and moral responsibility) to do it.

Anyone can appreciate the inconsistencies in group relationships. For instance, many groups make the mistake of casting all members in a similar mold, when in fact each of them is a unique individual. Another error is making rules that may cover the majority–the greatest good for the greatest number–but do not necessarily work for everyone. Still another is ascribing to

---

[1] A few individuals who have made a difference: Agnes Bojaxhiu, Aristotle, Bach, Churchill, Columbus, Curie, Darwin, Edison, Einstein, Ford, Gandhi, Hitler, Jesus, MLK, Jr., Lincoln, Marx, Muhammad, Newton, Pasteur, Plato, Shakespeare, da Vinci, Washington

others authority that ought to be retained by individuals. There are more, but these will serve for now.

Anyone can learn from the concept of community and its vital relationships. Community works because it provides many of the benefits of the group while also providing the necessary connection with mankind.

But in order to invoke community, we first must embrace morality because community is an ethical entity. It all rests on morality—honesty—and its extension, trust. And morality springs from ethics, which is founded in truth. If people embrace truth and deal with others honestly, sooner or later others will choose to trust them. And the process is repeated.

Any act of immorality reverses the process. Any attempt to make us alike or equal is an immoral act in itself. Why? Because it opposes a given. We already are equal and cannot be other than unique. There are givens, like it or not, and uniqueness and equality are among them.

Every group, including society, contains the seeds of its own demise, so we must individually transcend our society not only in our own interest, but in that of humankind as well. So long as society's rules and values are consistent with truth and honesty we may follow and promote them, but when they are not, each of us— is ethically charged to not only *not* follow them, but to change them so that they are.

Any one of us, *including you*, can do this. A move toward perfection that any of us makes can only have a positive effect on mankind and will in turn benefit any worthy society within it. And it is easier for the individual to make such a move than it is for any group because, as we've seen, all you have to do is to make the choice and it's done. No convincing or cajoling others of what to do or how to do it, just make the choice individually.

As always, it begins with you, with your own unique intellect, intuition, instincts, interests, emotions and feelings.

Remember that you have access to the entire wisdom of mankind to choose from, and your intellect enables you to be creative with it.

You are the key to it all because you, not the group, are vital to humanity. You can think. You can intuit. *You can create*. You can relate to any other on a fundamental and equal basis, and that relationship will be greater than its parts. You have no limits within humanity (and humanity is limitless!); you can choose alone, and you can create change alone.

All you have to do is be ethical (truthful) and act morally (honestly). Begin with yourself and direct yourself. But remember, your influence is limited to *what you do*. If others choose otherwise, you cannot force the issue—you can only hope to influence it. So be it.

You are not limited by any group of which you may be a member. You can maintain (or reclaim) your *self* at any time. You can achieve excellence alone. And, because two connecting individuals equal more than the sum of their parts (1+1>2), you can control at least half of any relationship. This is real power! And it's yours! Respect it! Use it!

Start with yourself and with the givens–your gifts. Accept yourself for what you are, take responsibility for

by *who* you are and encourage others to be and do like-
wise. Just do it. From now on, be ethical.

Once you make the choice to be ethical, you have
no choice other than to act morally. Conversely, acting
morally will cause you to be ethical. And as we shall
see, morality provides the safety net for those instances
when you must be unethical. And, because you are not
perfect, you *will* be unethical.

WHAT?

You're admonishing me to be ethical and now you're
telling me that I can't? Well, sort of.... But before you
throw the book away, you might want to find out why,
and at the same time realize the benefits of your inexora-
ble link with humankind (it's your lifeline). It all makes
perfect sense. And besides, we're almost done here.

Mankind has always intuitively known that certain characteristics such as corruption, vice and obscen-
ity to be immoral. These and others like them have no
redeeming qualities and can only have damaging results
on humanity. (Interestingly enough they can work, tem-
porarily, in some group environments.) Other negative
characteristics may be less obvious—they spring from
feelings and may be mistakenly justified on the grounds
that feelings are, after all, involuntary and therefore
can't be wrong in and of themselves. For instance, it's
almost impossible to go about daily living without the
occasional feeling of anger or resentment, or of being
better than or jealous of someone else.

However, while feelings themselves are not immoral,
how you deal with them may be. What you are (per-

haps even how you feel) may be beyond your control, but what you do remains your responsibility. You choose how to act on your feelings and emotions; you alone are responsible for the choices you make, and your responsibility to humanity requires that you act morally.

Acting otherwise—in opposition to the benefit of mankind—is what makes an action immoral.

You can deal effectively with many conflicts by simply reverting to *self*. If you appreciate and value your own individuality and that of others, you cannot violate someone else's being in any way. And endeavoring to do no harm will go a long way toward extending your ethical being outward into your relationships.

Even if you deal effectively with your feelings, there may come a time when you will lie. You may simply make a mistake. Considering the number of groups and their rules, some of which have become law, you may find it necessary to break those rules from time to time in order to maintain your own integrity or serve the greater good of humanity. Or it may be necessary to deal with an immoral individual on his terms rather than your own (perhaps to save a life—even your own). You can think of some examples.

In other words, despite your best intentions, you will compromise your efforts to be perfect. The fact that none of us are (perfect) should bring some comfort.

This clearly presents a quandary: how can a person be ethical if he is imperfect, or has no control over what may be dishonest feelings, or is forced to behave unethically? Because truth and perfection are concurrent concepts, and none of us are perfect, it should come as no surprise that he can't.

So long as groups dominate, none of us can be ethical all the time. Does this mean we ultimately must fail?

By no means. The solution to this dilemma points up a distinction between ethics and morality, at the same time providing a most valuable insight into the vital bond between the individual and humanity.

While we may find ourselves to be unethical (which may be difficult to admit, and which in turn may cause us to make excuses, even to the point of redefining ethics to suit the situation,) we need not act immorally.

Morality provides the means by which you can resolve your personal quandary. Humanity, in its wholeness and consummate wisdom, can save each of us from ourselves! The following answer is not ambiguous. It only serves to point up a subtle distinction between ethics and morality:

If you must be unethical, be honest about it.

Whoa! Does this mean that you can go through life doing whatever you wish at the expense of others, honestly admitting to being unethical? Of course not. If you did, you would be acting in a manner detrimental to humankind—immorally. It *does* mean that if (when) you find yourself in violation of ethics, admit it honestly, accept responsibility for it and resolve it in the best interest of mankind. It means that by being honest you are acting morally. It means that by being honest you will tend to resolve the issue in the best interest of mankind and in so doing enhance both humanity and yourself. No one could do more.

We noted earlier that acting in opposition to humankind is what makes an action immoral. We also listed some negative qualities universally acknowledged to act in opposition to humanity. Those qualities are destructive because they are affronts to both individual and humanity. Some are so much so that many groups, our society included, have enacted laws protecting us from them.

Other affronts to humanity are less public, more individual. Such basic violations of moral principle are immoral by virtue of being unethical. Some of these—apathy, arrogance, envy, greed—tend to be personal; others—hostility, jealousy, lewdness—may be more outward-directed.

It's illuminating to note that few laws protect us from personal affronts. Why? Simply because personal affronts are not group-oriented! Since they are impossible to even define by the group in the context of the group to the satisfaction of the group, they are of necessity largely ignored by the group.

Society and its laws step in when, for example, hostility results in damage to the group, or jealousy leads to a social crime, or lewdness leads to public abuse, or greed leads to thievery. Society doesn't attempt to outlaw such things as envy, apathy or arrogance, because 1) it can't; and 2) these don't appear to directly impinge on society as a group. Indeed, they may even be interpreted to number among our rights as individuals. But because society cannot deal with these things does not make them *rights,* or even right.

These negative qualities cannot be right(s) because they violate moral/ethical principles. They dishonor a member of humanity, they defile a *self*. And while they may be, by default or even fiat, our privileges, they are not rights. They are, in fact, quite the opposite. They are *wrong*s.

Because the group can't deal with some aspects of immorality does not mean that they need not be dealt with. They must be dealt with, and it falls upon the individual to deal with them.

The individual, not the group, can and must speak not only for himself but for all of humanity in matters involving ethics. It is the individual's duty to do so, his end of the same bond by which he was born and through which humanity comes to his rescue when he must be unethical. This, the substance of morality, illustrates the primacy of the individual. It's up to you.

When society and its laws, however sublime, fail (and they must),

IT IS UP TO YOU

CHAPTER SIX

Doing It – Living The Good Life

W e've correctly identified the individual—you—as the primary agent of change in humanity. We also know that no individual can operate in a vacuum, and we can appreciate that anarchy is not an option. Individual autonomy is your route to the good life. Autonomy not only considers mankind but presupposes it; therefore, it has a moral basis.

In order to achieve the good life, you need only believe what you already know and become who you already are; then *be* ethical and *act* morally. But is it possible to do this when everywhere we seem to be stymied by different sets of laws, values and morals that contradict the system of universal moral principles?

Absolutely! It simply means acting in conformity with truth, and truth, a given, can be chosen by anyone at any time. It simply requires using all the givens at your disposal.

But what about the law? Don't we have to obey the law as well?

Certainly, but which law? Here's the good news: there's much less to law than that spelled out in endless detail in volume upon volume of text, statute, ordinance, regulation and the like. In fact, if you are ethical and act morally, you also will be obeying all the law that really matters - *Natural Law.*

The Law That Matters – Natural Law

There's a universal standard that must be upheld by each and every one of us because we are interdependent. This standard applies to humanity as well as to all groups whether or not they acknowledge, endorse or even know about it. Like our lives, the sunrise and gravity, it's a given. It is integral with ethics, part of the system of universal moral principles, and it is implicit in our legal system. *Natural Law, a body of unchanging moral principles regarded as a basis for all human conduct,* puts the irrefutable law that matters on your side.

Our civil and criminal laws are inventions to satisfy particular needs of our society. Moral law, on the other hand, consists of basic ethical principles that describe generic right conduct by which our actions conform in our dealings with each other. These ethical standards are constant and immutable. They are givens.

And all law—including moral law and positive law—is rooted in Natural Law. Natural Law includes fundamental ideas of right and wrong that exist in and of humanity and implicit in moral law, even if not explicit in positive law. It precedes our very being, valid whether or not we or our society approve of or even acknowledge it. It is analogous with First Principles like truth.

And it represents the ultimate weapon of the individual. It's the Power of One.

Natural Law is fundamental, a given, an integral part of humanity. Individuals, groups, whole societies and mankind itself are subject to it. Its power is such that a person not only has a right to ascertain the virtue of institutional law, ethically he must do so. Conscience and intuition, unequivocally personal attributes independent of anyone else's influence (and anathema to many groups) are the ultimate deciding ethical factors. Such is the power and the responsibility of the individual. Your power.

That it may be ignored or even outlawed by a group or society itself does not change natural law's existence or power. It's there for our appreciation and application simply by acknowledging it. To deny it is immoral. The good life is impossible without it, just as humanity is impossible without water and sunlight. Sometimes, however, groups (including society itself) may try to circumvent natural law in their own interests. In doing so, they risk taking part in their own eventual demise.

The fact is that *no* group, our state-of-the-art society included, may speak for the whole of humanity. And while it may be the stated goal of our laws to achieve the right results for our society; that goal may not always be realized. On the other hand, moral law and natural law must, by the fact that they are givens, achieve the right (true, good, ethical) results for not only our society but for all of humankind, and this law is available to each one of us, individually, without benefit of any group.

It is this primal moral and natural law that provides our first line of (ethical) offense. It provides the means by which any individual, including you, can speak for humanity itself, and can ethically and legally resolve any problem.

One reason why each of us individually is here in the first place is to reaffirm those universal truths that give meaning to humanity and in so doing, move mankind forward.

This simply means that as you move toward your good life, you are at the same time moving forward the entire human race! In the process of improving yourself, you are making the world a better place for everyone. Further, since individuals have the tacit backing of an ethical whole–mankind in its entirety–through this vital connection, when you decide to accept your sole responsibility as a human being (to move mankind forward to the next level), *you can't lose.*

The system of principles that we have defined is, in essence, ethics, and the very practical issue we have chosen to describe is called living. This is not surprising, since ethics is, and always has been, an integral part of the good life. It defines it, in fact. The philosophy we're talking about here is nothing more than the system of universal moral principles. We have in fact articulated, in the context of life, what to do and how to do it. Legally.

You already knew all of this before you picked up this book. It came with your being. You had only to make the choice to accept it. Hopefully the perspective into which it's been placed here will help persuade you to make that choice, but no matter—you can make the choice to do it at any time. Results are guaranteed.

Simply stated, stick with the truth and act honestly. Realize your vital relationships; deal with others as you would be dealt with by others, and do no harm. By doing so you will live, create and progress. By simply being ethical, you will be complete, a fulfilled and integral part of humanity.

No group, however large, powerful or vocal can do this for you, nor does it have the power to divert you from the ethical line. Not only is it possible to be ethical alone, it's easier to understand your emotions and feelings, think individually, make conscious choices and accept personal responsibility alone than as part of a group. Use your rights, embrace morality and invoke community.

Do what's right, and change what's wrong. It's within your power and responsibility to do so.

You can stop right here and get to it or you may continue reading. But be warned: To go further requires abandoning the security of our material world, taking leave of your senses(!) and leaping off into the uncharted void. If you're game, read on.

PART TWO

A New Perspective: Thinking Creatively

CHAPTER SEVEN

Exploring Space - Looking For What Really Matters

Remember that any group, no matter its size, can occupy only its own little piece of the universe. There has to be *space* between entities. That space, in fact, connects with all other spaces (and space itself). And it is this space–not matter–that connects the universe and everything in it. Obviously it must have significance, and that significance is, like space itself, *endless*.

Things are discrete, separated by the continuous space between them. Once in that space we can move freely between those things, at the same time keeping our connection with the entire universe.

Once in the spaces you'll appreciate not only what's there but what isn't. And that's where you'll find not only autonomy and freedom but success–in those spaces that are so easy to ignore. If this isn't particularly clear, what follows should help.

Nothing Matters

Everything, including *nothing*, has significance, whether we see it, appreciate it, or even know about it. It's a fact that everything that ever was, even if we can find no trace of it, has resulted in *now*, has had an impact on *now*, and therefore matters *now*, because *now* is a direct result of all of it, including all the nothing of it.

And until we acknowledge that *nothing* matters, we will fail to realize one of our most productive resources.

It certainly matters to computers operating on the binary system—ones and zeroes (nothing), or, if you prefer, on and off. The only real unit in the entire system is one (unity), but it requires the nothing of zero (space) to function.

It's human nature to ignore many truths and facts–nothing being one of them–as a matter of course. For instance, when we look at this page, we see its height and width. But what we see in two dimensions also has a third– thickness–or it couldn't exist. But in this case thickness doesn't register. Without thinking, we very effectively ignore one of the basic requirements for it to even *be*. Two dimensions are enough.

Everyone knows what a line is without even considering that it's not a real thing at all. A line is a concept–imaginary–that has only one dimension: length. But we pass over this fact because only that one dimension matters to us–the other two do not. But there's even less...

A point is dimensionless, an *idea* representing among other things the cross-section of a one-dimensional line, so it has none of the three dimensions necessary for it to exist. But here again, dimensions don't matter to us. We've effectively eliminated every one of them and still feel totally in touch with reality. Do you see where we're going with this?

Because there's still less. Consider the space between objects. Nothing's there, yet it registers on us just as surely as if something were. Its nothingness means something to us.

If it (whatever *it* is) isn't there, and we not only recognize it but can measure it, then it must have some degree of importance. It must matter. And if nothing is included among these concepts, it follows that *nothing matters.*

If this strikes you as pointless nattering, stay with me for a few more paragraphs. I promise to make my point (dimensionless pun intended...).

Most of what we think of as matter—even a block of lead—is largely space. Subatomic particles move (very rapidly) in the spaces between themselves. Because we can hardly lift this "solid" mass of dense "inert" matter doesn't change the fact that it's mostly space and motion. We might even say that the space within "solid" matter defines that matter as much as the particles making it up, just as the "blank" spaces around these letters and words you're reading define them perfectly.

Without the spaces around them there could be no letters. Each letter has a distinctive shape, matched perfectly by the space surrounding it. From this point of view, the space separating letters (and words) becomes just as important as the inked shapes themselves. The only thing connecting these letters is the continuous space between them. Boundaries join as well as separate.

Neighboring things hold a boundary in common—the boundary belongs to both. The edge of a letter is also the edge of the space around it. This edge is, in this respect, a unifying feature.

Look into the blank spaces between these letters under a microscope and you won't find *nothing*. The power of the microscope determines just how blank these "spaces" are not. And no matter how powerful the microscope, you'll find still more "space" to be examined by an even more powerful one. Greater magnification reveals that what seems to be decreasing space in fact increases proportionally, to be explored by even more powerful means. Where does it end?

We don't even know how to know, yet we behave as if we understood it perfectly, just like we deal with lines, points and nothing itself. *Without a thought.*

Without a thought is the operative phrase here, presaging what we'll be discussing from here on out. We don't consider that *nothing* has significance. We forget that boundaries join as well as separate; we stop at the boundaries–we forget to keep looking! But even without thinking, we move forward. Can there be more to it than we suppose?

In fact, there's more to it than we can possibly imagine. The point is that what we don't perceive arguably can be even more important as what we do perceive. Nothing (as in *no thing*) really does matter, and much of what we deal with on a daily basis consists of no thing.

A final thought regarding the importance of nothing: We all understand the meaning of the phrase: reading between the lines. To truly understand, we often have to examine the spaces as well. We know that the real meaning of someone's words is conveyed not by the words alone but also by the spaces, silences and pauses that accompany them. Ignoring these things can mask the essential meaning of those words and sentences. And we often do just that, because we're distracted by the sheer quantity of words.

And of things, as well. We have to get past the clutter and into those spaces–spaces between things and spaces between thoughts. Unless we do, we can't move freely. Whatever it is that we're looking for will be connected with those large and small spaces that are yet to be discovered and explored, those spaces that we look at but don't see. And the only route to any of it is through the spaces that join–as well as separate–them.

Spaces. Ignore them and live in the world we see. Explore them and discover the world that is.

Exploring Space

Groupthink suggests that anything worthwhile that could have been done *has* been done. All the letters, words and lines have been investigated, analyzed, deconstructed and reconstructed in any number of ways. Just move forward from where you are. Don't waste time backing up and reinventing the wheel.

Buying into groupthink is a bad idea. Groups push their own agendas, seeing only what they want to see, ignoring whatever doesn't promote whatever it is that they're getting done. But that which they've passed over just might have some value to the rest of us. By using our distinctive minds, we just may find a gem that others have overlooked.

And those gems are there. In order to find them we have to be willing to go beyond the physical "comfort zone" that science and other groups have defined for us, and into the largely unexplored spaces large and small that define us in ways we have yet to discover. Getting into them uses resources usually either taken for granted or ignored.

We know that we're not just a collection of physical parts. While our bodies are mostly water and space, for some reason "it works for us." Why? Because we're more than mere matter. There are dimensions to us beyond what we can see, or even imagine.

We have minds that enable us to get outside of ourselves and into those spaces. Remember imagination, that intangible enabling us to conceive of what's neither present nor possible? And intuition, another abstraction by which we can perceive truth without reasoning? These aren't things, but they're available for us to use in our own unique ways. Remember also that human beings are creative; our minds do more than process information, they *generate* it.

Thought, whatever it may or may not be, is not matter. It's not a solid, or a liquid or, as some ancients hypothesized, a gas, but thought very clearly is more than nothing. It's a given, just like those spaces are. And it's universal and innate. You don't have to be taught to think. If you couldn't count on that, you couldn't count at all.

Mind may well be what some part of the brain does, but even if we explain thought and feelings away as cellular perturbations or electrical impulses, what causes or produces them? Are they self-generating or are they reactions? If they're reactions, to what? The answers to these questions remain for now in spaces yet to be found, let alone explored.

There is, in fact, a dimension to us not only beyond the physical, but beyond the mental as well. Ignoring for the moment how this could be–whether or not it is the result of some chemical reaction that was part of our natural evolution or something else entirely–return for a moment to the brain, that three-pound organ that is the boundary between our physical and extra-physical elements.

The largest part of the brain–the cerebrum–has two lobes. Does that mean we have two brains? In a way, yes. They are separate if not equal, and they interact. The left lobe handles rational and descriptive thinking, the right lobe directs the artistic and abstract functions that we can't quantify or even completely describe, ensuring our ability to imagine, intuit, exercise insight and appreciate intangibles like beauty, quality, liberty, virtue and character, along with the ability to combine disparate information from diverse sources, ideas that cannot be fully described but are understood on some level.

The left brain dominates and, historically, we are a left-brained world. (Even our educational systems are geared toward the rational left brain. Most subjects are verbal and numerical, while the arts are minimized.)

> Dr. Betty Edwards, an art professor at Cal State University, Long Beach, described in her books (about drawing) an almost mechanical approach toward making the switch from left to right brain that can be quickly learned by

almost anyone.[2] Her technique involves defining the nothing to let the objects emerge—a method of drawing the spaces rather than the objects themselves (it seems that nothing matters here as well). Try it. It works.

The Brain

Left Hemisphere	Right Hemisphere
Quantitative	Qualitative
Scientific	Metaphysical
Routine	Creative
Real	Abstract
Rational	Intuitive
Objective	Subjective
Thinking	Feeling
Digital	Analog
Time	Space
Learn	***KNOW***

Look at the last word on the list above. It's a fact that *you can't know something that isn't true.* Knowing is the final step of learning. When you *KNOW,* you have the facts…and that's what we're after—facts. How do we get them?

Our left brain does a great job. It does it so well that we tend to forget about its silent partner that enables it in the first place. This bias causes many of the difficulties we meet when trying to get beyond

---

[2]   Edwards, Betty: Drawing on the Right Side of the Brain 1979 Penguin-Random House NY

what we can see. Yet if we are to explore the spaces we have to somehow tap into the intuitive strengths of the right brain as well as the rational ones of the left. The right half tends to rely on intangibles (feelings, hunches) rather than disciplined logic and the burden of weighing out the pros and cons. It's better at such things as discrimination of shapes and expressing emotion. Its resources can be employed much more effectively than they have been. It's time to use what the whole brain has to offer.

Once we choose to employ the entire brain to look beyond (or in the spaces between) the physical environment that daily overwhelms our five senses, we can begin to expand our horizons.

Beyond Mind

Our minds combine real and imagined data, random associations, unique experiences and every other input seen or unseen, heard or unheard, touched or untouched, smelled or odorless. The process doesn't follow a direct path from here to there, but adapts with every new connection, unplanned but not random, moving unalterably toward its only goal—more. Neither communal nor predictable, it constantly, automatically and individually just *becomes*. And you cannot stop it!

Ideas and creativity are products of mind, and something more. Mind, remember, is how the brain enables thought. Among other things, mind makes it possible to articulate and communicate intangibles to others by some process whereby they can know what we mean.

Until now we've largely cast our lot with science/technology and its singular preoccupation with the physical world as defined in its own terms. In order to proceed further we should take a fresh look at philosophy and in particular, metaphysics.

Scientific principle includes a handful of laws that are really assumptions–no more than known truths that cannot be proven, which you will recognize as givens. Science has no answers to gravity and electromagnetism,. We know they exist, but why? Science requires proof. We need to go beyond the need for proof. We need to explore the *irrational*. This is the realm of metaphysics. (Metaphysics will be discussed briefly in Chapter 10, and extensively in Part Three.)

CHAPTER EIGHT

Philosophy And The World Beyond
Something To Think About

Philosophy historically has worked to explain or justify in some way what may well seem to be intellectually untenable. Let's take a closer look at this arcane approach to answering a chronic need of mankind.

Apparently the need to explore our extra-physical (supernatural?) nature and provide explanations for mysteries that couldn't be explained in any other way is as old as mankind itself. While science has solved many of these mysteries, others remain beyond our comprehension. Still, convinced that the rest of the answers lie just around the next scientific corner, many have abandoned philosophy to put their effort into the hard science that seems to serve us so well. In fact, our own society has all but purged philosophy from its operating system. In so doing it has limited our access to a valuable, time-honored resource.

Our civil law has ordained that spiritual abstraction has no place in its system of regulation, on the strength of its being properly directed (by our Constitution) that government has no place in religion. Thus our society has mistakenly and improperly assigned much of philosophic thinking to the realm of religion. Big mistake. In that process it throws out the baby with the bathwater.

The fault is not entirely society's; philosophy shares the blame. One reason is a pervasive tendency of groups to employ proprietary jargon; new words (including many *–isms*) invented in philosophy's behalf effectively separate it from the mainstream. Another reason is an unfortunate tendency of some philosophers to support their inquiries by employing scientific methodology (in some cases even—purely mathematical methods have been applied). This ill-advised and self-defeating backward step cannot work because, as stated earlier, science is a *product* of metaphysics and cannot be used to prove or disprove that from which it came. However, the main reason probably is that philosophy has shifted from its original inquiries (into pure knowledge–*truth*) to a game played among intellectuals intent on their own individual agendas.

While they may begin as legitimate courses of objective individual inquiry, philosophies become increasingly directed and specialized as they are absorbed by groups. These groups take a stand, decide upon a system incorporating their values, establish a hierarchy, and forge their own sets of rules. And, like many groups, they become their own agendas.

Organized philosophies suffer from the same problems as any group. They begin to serve the logic of their systems rather than the aims of all mankind.

Their knowledge becomes proprietary; they gather at universities and pursue their own agendas with growing intensity as they move further and further from their original purposes.

And should the prevailing society see the actions of any group as a challenge to its own preeminence, there's a good chance that it will take steps to restrain that group. Any group that develops an agenda in conflict with that of the governing society runs the risk of censorship, and not without good reason. Remember, groups are not created equal. In spite of what may be good intentions, their agendas may be inappropriate to what society sees as the greatest good for its greatest number.

Ethics and the moral code traditionally (and rightfully) have been the province of philosophy. But when society arbitrarily assigns philosophy to the realm of religion and then nullifies it on the basis of mutual exclusivity with its laws, morality suffers and so does the society it seeks to serve. We may argue whose fault it is, but the loss is ours, individually. This constitutes a real problem that only the individual (you again) can solve.

At the very least there has to be individual inquiry into ethics and morality because moral principle is not a product of utilitarian or humanistic ideology if only because it's not a product at all. Society won't do it and even religious groups can't do it. We're back to the individual—you.

So what can *you* do? Go beyond the system, that's what.

Beyond Science

We've seen how we as individuals mature through a series of stages from total dependency through some degree of independency to interdependency as we grow intellectually by way of education, observation, experience and random thought processes. At the same time we are reinforced in spite of ourselves by the phenomena of connection and progression. We are ever-changing, always expanding our own envelope. By opening ourselves to the metaphysical resources available to every one of us we can blow the lid off mere scientific progress.

But first we have to be willing to explore dimensions beyond the mind, and to persuade ourselves that it's OK to proceed without the proofs and guarantees demanded by our current notion of science and the groups that dominate our culture. We must be willing to break free of the self-imposed bonds of the scientific method. And we must be willing to go it alone. How? Beyond the requirement of some level of maturity, it's simple. Choose, and trust.

Mankind continues to make progress despite what we do to impede it. From the days when almost everything was dealt with in terms of physical survival, we've been moving toward a future where ideas increasingly predominate. We haven't seen the end of it–it still has a long way to go. This natural progression, automatic and demonstrable, is not necessarily linear, or even logical and rational, for that matter.

We're treading boggy ground here, a realm that our secular, scientifically oriented society has improperly assigned to religious thinking. But religion is not the issue. Religions themselves are institutions, and as such are not permanent. While we've been conditioned to think that anything dealing with ethics and morality must have religious underpinnings, this is not the case. It's *philosophy*, that same philosophy that spawned our beloved science. But, because of how groupthink has affected our own thinking, it will take some discussion of extra-physical phenomena to put it straight.

Belief Systems

Not many years ago some degree of spirituality was both fashionable and widespread–our founding fathers, in fact, assumed it (and employed it in writing our founding documents). Mankind almost certainly has had some sort of "set of beliefs concerning the cause, nature and purpose of the universe" for far longer than its 5000 years of recorded history. It is, in fact, innate (could it be a *given?*) Early mystics attributed phenomena such as the movements of the stars and planets to the work of beings with supernatural powers. Various mysterious entities–gods–ran the machinery of the heavens, earth and seas, and man sought to avoid being caught up and destroyed by these awesome powers by explaining them as best he could. With the passage of time, and progress fueled by increased knowledge and understanding, this early mysticism became more structured and academic. Some of the resulting sets of beliefs—philosophies—developed into religions, each with its own theology. And each with its own agenda.

And right along with this development came insti-tutions–particular groups we call churches–each with *its* own theology, agenda and hierarchy.

But while mysticism virtually disappeared from public view with the onset of science, spiritualty did not. Even our own society's conviction that the rest of the answers lie just around the next scientific corner has not persuaded many of its number to abandon spiritual-ity. But if science is physical and therefore self-limiting, philosophy is not. Neither mankind nor its philosophies are prisoners of science's logic or proofs. Our science is simply the latest attempt to explain things rationally as best we can. But there remains an urgency that rational-ity and logic cannot satisfy. That there's more to life than institutions has always been known, if not acknowl-edged. It is, in fact, intuitive to each of us. A given.

Even though we might know the answer in terms of the words describing it, the meaning of life (living) and its purpose (creating) remain enigmatic abstrac-tions. Our lives may be givens, but our comprehension of them is not. Each of us has to figure out his own life as it unfolds and invents itself (and many of us never do). Doing so requires trust—belief—as well as rea-son. And no group can dictate what to believe, because belief is wholly personal.

Just as science isn't the ultimate arbiter of truth, neither is any organized philosophy the arbiter of belief. The best that any group can do is to accomplish the task for which it was organized. Only mankind is capable of everything, and you have all of mankind's resources at your disposal.

The function of mankind is to be, become and create. And that, precisely, is your function as well. That requires, in the absence of sufficient current knowledge, *belief.* You can choose to believe or not but choosing the negative will cut you off from what could be out there. And know this: *it's out there.*

Creating Your Personal Belief System

Trusting in the extra-physical is not confined to religious groups. Trust is personal, not institutional, and you, whether or not you admit it, have some measure of it.

Using the doctrines of any group to substitute for your own personal knowledge or belief system runs the same risk as any group approach–the greatest good for the greatest number of the group. Identifying only with a group may very well confine you to its baseline, which may be incomplete or even erroneous. Better to identify with a group after you have shaped your own beliefs. That way you bring your ideas to the group rather than being held to its dogma. No group has all of the answers. Only mankind in its entirety has them, and you have free access to all of it on the spiritual/metaphysical level.

Creating your individual belief system requires only your *choice* to do so; it doesn't require that any institution confirm it. It requires simply that you start with the givens available to us all and choose only truth from there on out. If you are honest and sincere in your effort, you will arrive at a point that few groups can reach, and none can surpass.

The hardest part is to ignore or avoid groupthink. There's always a group ready and willing to tell you what to believe. This problem can be avoided by–how else? –starting at the beginning. Start with the givens, and don't get derailed.

Sounds simple enough—just do it–but is it?

It's even simpler than that. It's automatic. Accepting it is, simply, *not* choosing to *not* accept it. You don't have to do anything at all. After all, you own your reality and all of its givens just by being here. Your being already acknowledges it; now just **believe what you know!**

The fact is, it takes a certain maturity to be able to ignore and move beyond what we see, hear, feel, taste and smell to consider the intangible yet no less real world that surrounds and even defines us just as space surrounds and defines matter. And while what's in our face can distract us and make this difficult, it's not impossible.

At this stage of our development, we can only move–automatically–in the direction of that understanding with no idea of what it holds or how distant from us it is. Mankind itself is doing exactly this–moving away from the largely sentient existence of our early ancestors toward a more metaphysical existence in spite of itself. There's no other way. It's a given, simply the way it is.

Like our minds, our lives are neither logical nor planned, nor are they mapped out for us. Each of us invents—**creates**—our own life as we live it, thereby helping create the world as well.

Beginning with our own conception, much of each of our individual lives is accidental, a response to apparently random happenings and circumstances over which we had no control but to which we constantly adapt in our own unique way. It always progresses (that's a given). No matter how we strive for a perfection that we cannot achieve at our present level of knowledge, there simply are too many subtle variables that we don't know about, let alone understand. At this stage of our development, we can only move–naturally–in the direction of that understanding with no idea of what it holds or how distant from us it is. Mankind itself is doing exactly this–moving away from the largely sentient existence of our early ancestors toward a more metaphysical existence in spite of itself. There's no other way. It's a given, simply the way it is.

Belief (Or Conviction, Or Trust, Or…)
The Givens, Again

Just what do you believe? All of the givens we've mentioned throughout the course of this book are worthy of your belief, because they *are*, like it or not. And there are more. It's really a matter of **accepting *what is***. Anything more runs the risk of error. Anything less is crippling.

And you can call it whatever you choose, if not belief or trust. If none of these work for you, even acknowledgment will do for starters.

In any case, real living requires a conviction beyond the physical and sentient. Merely accepting life requires trusting that our reactions to what happens from one moment to the next (rather than futilely trying to plan each move) often is as much as we can do, and it's certainly appropriate. This trust is, in fact, a necessary condition of life, and you already have it. Consider: you believe that you will be alive in the next instant, otherwise why would you bother surviving this one? You go to sleep fully expecting–trusting–that you will awaken alive. The fact is, accept it or not, you *believe* it. You accept it unconditionally, even though you can't prove it. Just another given.

While there are any number of givens to accept and believe, actually making the commitment to trust in them is a matter of individual intellectual choice. You may, but don't have to, do so. However, if you wish to use your own resources to move beyond what others would lead you to believe (in other words, *if you would think for yourself and grow as a human being*), there's no better alternative than to begin by trusting in *what is*. Any limitations placed on the givens are self-inflicted. Many are without explanation and beyond understanding; however, that does not in any way invalidate them. There are many things that we can't know. For instance:

Why a particular egg cell was fertilized by a particular sperm cell so that *you*, particularly, were born? Such questions will go unanswered, but do they matter? You bet they do because they concern you. But it has to remain enough at this point to merely trust in them and acknowledge our inability to explain them.

These last few paragraphs are meant to hammer home a point and to highlight the impetus driving philosophy and other intellectual pursuits created in man's ongoing attempt to explain the unexplainable. Now it's time to take a closer look at that chronic need of mankind...

Trust

Beyond your being here and the givens that you can count on no matter what, you might wish to have something else on which to hang your hat, and the physical world we live in would seem to be a solid beginning. Let's start at its beginning, which just happens to be the beginning of time as we know it.

The Big Bang is the theory *du jour* about the beginnings of our universe that satisfies most of the scientific community because it makes sense and parts of it can be proven. Basically it says that the universe began about 14-billion years ago as a result of a glitch whereby mass (no less than the entire mass of all that makes up the universe) was created, virtually instantaneously and totally, from ...what? Nothing? Some kind of energy? This theory begs questions like: *Huh? Glitch?* And possibly, *How?* Maybe even *Why?* Where did this energy come from? Why was it there? How long had it been there? Always (just how long is that?) or since when? Actually, science suggests some answers, but for now let's just say that "it" had to be there prior to a Big Bang.

It follows that this primal singularity must have included the source of what followed: things both material and not (like our minds). Further, there's no real reason to doubt that traces of it still exist. Since it's timeless...

Please realize that we're dealing with a subject that can't possibly be resolved at this time. We can't use the outcome to prove its source any more than we can use science to prove its source or words to prove reality.

We can't begin to explain the origins of that initial something/nothing that fuels our existence. There's no standard by which to even estimate it, nor do we know that a comprehensible standard is even possible. We don't even have the words to articulate it. For instance: Because of the non-existence of time before the Big Bang (our very concept of time depends on matter in motion, so time in our terms could not have existed before matter), that singularity must be by definition ageless, dateless, timeless and continuous. By definition we could say, for now at least, that if not infinite, it certainly could be eternal and immortal, maybe even *instantaneous*. What do these words mean to you?

Further to the point: we can't use the term energy because it has a scientific definition that can't be used to define its precursor. Similarly, force is an engineering term that would seem to preclude its use as well, although it's been used before with some success. It is perhaps best described by the philosophical term *dynamis*, which will have to suffice here.

It may come as a surprise that this suggestion of some eternal singularity (and the spiritual overtones accompanying it) springs from the very science that often seems bent upon proving otherwise. Actually, it shouldn't be surprising because no less than Isaac Newton, arguably the most brilliant and influential scientific mind of his time (possibly *ever*, for that matter), attributed the omnipotence of God to the order he discovered in the laws of gravity and the mathematics of motion as he laid waste to Cartesian rationalism. What does seem strange is that his discoveries were in large part responsible for the secularism springing from that very spiritual enlightenment that spawned modern science. It really comes down to that very subject of belief that we're investigating here: *trust*.

At any rate, we may state with some certainty that whatever preceded the universe not only still pervades everything in it (and perhaps–why not– beyond?), but also is continuous within all matter. It exists in an unbroken continuum between quarks, solar systems, constellations and galaxies. It was, is, and will be, at least until the end (if there *is* one) of the entire system that contains it. Disbelieving or not accepting this potency doesn't change it: if the Big Bang makes any sense, so also does the idea that we must be given of it and whatever preceded it.

So the stuff of religious philosophy, at least in this context, turns out to be no more or less than assigning the *dynamis* preceding the universe to some entity, power, force or what have you that precedes our world (or universe, or whatever unit you choose as your base). This singularity is universally continuous from mankind's point of view–a given. It was, is, and, as far as we can know, will be. It is ageless, dateless, timeless, eternal, immortal, all-being and unproveable. Given these parameters, many religious philosophies choose to equate it (along with Newton) with an all-powerful supreme entity.

In the absence of scientific proof (impossible at this stage of our development), many of the world's religions ask that you trust in some higher power having created the universe. All they've really done is to put the Big Bang into a perspective that might be grasped by those they sought to inform. Their "creator" is defined as eternal (ageless, dateless, timeless), whatever this term may truly mean. Since everything, including each of us, is a result of that primal force; we must all be part of it. Are they wrong? Was Newton wrong? You don't know, and neither do I.

Without making judgment as to the validity of any particular religious belief, it seems clear that for there to be a universe at all, there must at least be some primal potentiality beyond our current ability to comprehend. We may debate its origins or purpose, but it is reasonable that it was, and is, there, and scientifically consistent with the Big Bang, as far as science can go with it.

While we're in the frame of reference of eternal potentiality, we may as well consider the *eternal* part of it. The concept of eternity can boggle the mind but, like infinity, it too is scientifically consistent in spite of our finding it difficult to visualize, much less fathom, space curved by gravity or a line with no beginning and no end that extends, as it were, forever. Forever implies time (which we can comprehend, at least insofar as it enables us to deal with one thing following the next), which in turn leads to infinite time or timelessness, which we *cannot* comprehend. While we can measure time in whatever units we choose (say a lifetime), how can we deal reasonably with a concurrent timelessness? Mind-boggling.

Choose your belief. It really doesn't matter which one you select. Because whatever is true is the way it is, no matter what you, or I, or any of us think. Which is exactly the point.

We're at a point beyond which our science, sensory systems, rationality, logic and known dimensions can't take us at the speed to which we've become accustomed. At this point in our human development we can't possibly truly conceive of–much less explain–a timeless and dimensionless potentiality in terms that we can rationally deal with. We are at the point where, in order to understand further, we have to trust. We have to assume, just as we, and science, always do and always have done. We have to make, for want of a better expression, a leap of faith. We have to accept the fact that there are things that, although we can and do depend on for our very existence, we can't fully understand. We have to acknowledge that there may be other dimensions beyond those which we can conceive. We have to know that we do not know. Some choose to *believe*. And no matter how many of us deny it, and how emphatically we deny it, collectively, we do.

CHAPTER NINE

Believe What You Already Know and Become Who You Already Are

While mind is how the brain relates each individual beyond himself, its use necessarily is limited to terms that its owner can deal with. While our minds require our brains, the ubiquitous potency of the universe does not. In other words, there remains a dimension of universal potency that is the essence of our existence, a vital incorporeal part of life itself that pervades our being. It exists within us as well as in all of space without us, connecting each of us to not only every other one of us, but to every corner of the universe, perhaps beyond.

This *essence* is original, eternal and immortal, meaning simply that it was here before us and will not cease at our death, and any failure to acknowledge it does not negate it. Because it is not only real but the source of all that follows, it enables whatever follows. That we possess intelligence does not preclude the possibility of that same intelligence, even something superior to it, existing elsewhere (everywhere?), wherever that may be. Nor does the fact that we utilize this essence in a way that serves our particular purpose make it our exclusive possession or preclude its universal existence beyond us.

It is our particular part of this vital essence intrinsic to humanity that inspires and animates each and every human being, that enables our own thoughts, feelings and actions that concerns us directly. Specifically, it's what connects each one of us, individually, with the rest of mankind and, in fact, with the universe.

My dictionary defines *spirit* as "the principle of conscious life; the vital principle in humans; the incorporeal part of humans; conscious incorporeal being, as opposed to matter," that which inspires, animates and pervades being–thought, feeling, action. I suggest that spirit is the vital essence, although consciousness might do as well. I offer as well the term *soul* to represent this spirit in individual human terms, that part of spirit which resides in the spaces integral to our individual selves.

If it's uncomfortable to apply these terms in a secular way, so be it. Inventing a new term would serve no useful purpose. Certainly no religious nuance is intended here (compare with the ideas of Plotinus, a Third Century pagan—and therefore clearly secular—intellectual). Any problem lies with a predisposition to reject things other than what we can see—because logic, science and rationality are not comprehensive enough to effectively deal with concepts beyond their realm. We need something more. We need trust. And most importantly we need trust in our *selves*.

Maturity Revisited

Earlier we said that some degree of maturity is necessary to put this stuff to work. In fact, maturity as earlier defined can fall short of what's required. What's really necessary is some degree of spiritual (in terms of the previous definition) development, an ongoing, never-ending, maturation process. Once you reach so-called "maturity," you're only partway there. You have to continue growing even after you realize that you are expanding along with the universe itself.

John J. Goetz, in his research and writing in urban studies (1989, personal communication), has enumerated certain characteristics of mature individuals who continue to grow as human beings:

- they do not always put themselves first;
- they relate well to others, and treat others as individuals;
- they seek the ultimate well-being of others in addition to their own;
- they realize their limited abilities and see value in a diversity of talents and backgrounds;
- they are able to discern, to see past words spoken to what really is being said; they keep themselves under control; and
- they recognize that groups exist to fill a social need;

These are characteristics that we've covered in preceding pages, but there's one more:

Mature individuals recognize that they are not the end-all, but are answerable to higher authority.

Such people cannot stop growing because they know that they are connected in some way with the universe, and therefore to everyone else.

Your Essence: Your Personal *Nothing Matters*

As an integral part of humanity, you are vitally connected to it and the rest of the universe as well. And, space and energy being continuous, it should be obvious that part of that very space and energy resides as well in every part of the universe, including each one of us. It follows that whatever happens in any part of this continuum is connected, however indirectly, to every corner of the universe, however large. The following statement was made much earlier; now, however, it's offered here from a more aggressive perspective:

You matter, regardless of how infinitesimal you believe your effect to be, and you do not, and cannot, know how much, or little, that may be.

But the fact that you are connected does not guarantee that you'll take advantage of all that it really means to you. It's up to you to realize your relevance and make a difference. How? By getting into those spaces, of course, the spaces that truly connect us. In order to go beyond ourselves, our brains and our minds, we have to get beyond the physical limits that we have set on them and when we do, to assent to an infinite and eternal connection. You simply(?) get in touch with your soul, that individual connection with the spiritual and the cosmos. And you don't have to go to church to do it.

Unless you're willing to move beyond the logical and rational, beyond science and its limited methodology, even beyond thinking, you risk remaining locked into only what you can see. To move beyond that point you have to be willing to go beyond the limits imposed by conscious thought. You have to know that a verity need not be verified. You have to trust in the concept of spirit. The only thing you really have to do is to *know the truth*. It will indeed set you free. And truth is always there–a given–absolute. Finding it is something else.

Beyond Reason

Abandoning reason might seem to be a strange thing to ask of an intelligent person seeking truth, but before you make any rash judgments, consider again the surplus of things that we have no way of knowing using "conventional" wisdom, yet must have some grasp of, in order to move forward.

Also consider that, while we easily conceive of things to which we can relate, as well as the day-to-day process of living, our bodies cannot handle too much light or too much pain. Looking directly at the sun for even a few seconds can blind you forever. An excess of sound leads to pain, an excess of which can cause loss of consciousness and actual physical damage. Our bodies simply don't handle some physical things very well.

Even thought has its limits. We do not relate easily to concepts like eternity and infinity, space without mass or light, the absence of time, or beyond limits imposed by absolute zero or the speed of light. Nor do we truly comprehend insanity. Insane people do not function well in our society (nor we in theirs), so we separate them from us for their safety and protection (not to mention our own peace of mind). We minister to them as best we can, but we can never completely relate on a "normal" level because their "abnormal" thinking conflicts with our own "rational" thinking.

Some minds apparently operate on an "irrational" level. But for all we know, the minds of some of those we classify as psychiatric cases (autistic savants who can solve complex mathematical equations at a glance), are operating, to some degree at least, on another, possibly higher level.

Part of our reluctance to abandon rationality is a result of an uncomfortable uncertainty. In order to deal with these irrational things and situations, we may have to get, for want of a better term, beyond–out of–our minds. But before we tackle that rather unnerving concept, let's do a little more investigation regarding functions of our physical brains—specifically, the *subconscious.*

It's a fact that our brains continue to operate even when our bodies and minds are for all purposes inert— after all, brain functions are necessary to maintain life. Accepting that our minds continue to operate at some subconscious level shouldn't pose too much of a problem.

Look up its definition and you'll find subconscious equated with words like mind, self, instinct, intuition and the sublime, even spirit, all essential principles of our conscious life—appreciated or not—that we've dealt with in preceding pages, and all basic to our very humanity.

The subconscious (the source of inference) is common to all of humanity. It always operates, even when we're unaware. It's only in the realm beyond the rational that the ability to stop thinking has any meaning. And philosophy, in its concern with the metaphysical, should represent a legitimate course by which to move toward the supra-rational.

Humans are the only known beings able to look at themselves from outside themselves. Doing so enables us to develop insight and wisdom not available to other forms of life. This indeed is the reason that we can tap the vast store of information that comes with every one of us at birth. Doesn't it make sense to use these unique powers to investigate our reason for being? All you have to do is stop thinking, and perceive.

Stop thinking? Now there's a tall order. From the altogether left-brain point of view it doesn't make sense, no pun intended. After all, you usually know you're conscious because your mind is operating–that is, you're thinking. Just making the decision not to think requires thought. Only by being in some realm other than the rational does not thinking make any sense at all.

While it may seem irrational to think about not thinking, there remain techniques for opening your mind to input other than the sensible, many of which have their roots in Oriental philosophies. It requires opening your*self* to the sublime by "letting go." Any number of books have been written on the subject of transcending thought. Some are easier to read than others.

One way of transcending thought is to empty your mind of it–allow whatever comes into your mind to pass through without consciously processing it. No action, no comment, just let it be, and let it go. If it leaves tracks that have some impact on whatever you do or think subsequently, that's not important to the task at hand.

Emptying the mind of thought is not easy because we're so used to left-brain thinking that we are not comfortable when overriding the process. Although not analogous, it may help to consider it in terms of listening.

Real listening is possible only when you stop thinking and processing only what you are hearing even while the speaker is talking. Real listening requires total attention without personal thought. If you've never really listened (and a surprising number of us have not), try it to find out just how difficult it is.

But emptying your mind of thought and allowing ideas to pass through unheeded goes beyond listening in much the same way that metaphysics goes beyond physics. It demands total *in*attention, a literally *open mind* and total relaxation. It requires just *being*.

Stopping thinking involves the right brain and the subconscious interfacing with *the nothing-that-matters*, opening your mind to dimensions beyond it. But it's possible, and you can do it, alone. One formal method is Transcendental Meditation, sometimes done in a group, but remember to treat groups with caution. Better to go it alone.

Once you have totally opened your mind to the dimensions beyond it, you will have a better appreciation for the subconscious, the subliminal, and metaphysics. Your connection with mankind in its entirety will be enhanced. When you are able to transcend thought, you will make a connection beyond not only the physical, but beyond the mental. You will, in fact, experience an infinite and eternal spiritual connection, as well as a much deeper knowledge of your*self,* which will lead to a greater appreciation of others. Insight to the max.

Trusting in the extra-physical (spiritual conviction) has nothing to do with religion. It's really a very personal phenomenon connecting each of us with the whole of mankind and beyond. Remember, you can't confirm reality through any institution, not even a religious one. It takes a living thing to do that, and even religious groups are not vital. But you are.

Trusting in the extra-physical is simply a matter of taking advantage of the resources of humanity which, collectively, include all the answers. And accept it or not, you *are* connected to the entirety of humanity and the rest of the universe as well; therefore, you have access to all the answers. The Power of One is awesome.

Where does that leave us?

We've come full-circle. Starting with givens we have returned to givens. Starting with being we have returned to being. Only now we have considered even more givens, made the case that we do not have to understand them in order to accept them, and developed a new appreciation for the meaning of *being* itself. To review:

The function of humanity, and each of us individually, is to be, become and create. In addition to knowledge, this requires a belief inherent in every one of us, whether or not we acknowledge it. The givens, accepted or not, are given to everyone, believe it or not.

We each create our lives (givens) as we live them and live our lives as we create them. If you consider this fully, you might conclude that in doing so we are, each of us and collectively, not only confirming reality but *creating* it, and if this is true, it follows that we are in fact creating the future. You may wish to think about this for a moment…or more…

Science places the beginning of time (a given) as we know it at the Big Bang–some 13.7Billion years ago. Before that there was no time as we know it.

But some timeless (eternal) potency had existed even before that. It connects us all to all of mankind. And you have access to all wisdom by way of it.

Science and philosophy (including even the religious kind) converge at some point in the past, and since science is a product of philosophy, it may again in the future. You can either believe this or not, but failing to do so does not invalidate it. Whatever happened could have happened, and whatever will happen, *will* happen. It's happening now. Make it happen to you.

It all comes down to this: Since you are important you may as well take advantage and *be* important. Begin with the truth. You can do it at any time. Why not now?

Believe what you already know and
become who you already are.

PART THREE
The Age Of Mind

PROLOGUE

In Defense of Philosophy

Philosophy is to be studied, not for the sake of any definite answers to its questions since no definite answers can, as a rule, be known to be true, but rather for the sake of the questions themselves; because these questions enlarge our conception of what is possible, enrich our intellectual imagination and diminish the dogmatic assurance which closes the mind against speculation; but above all because, through the greatness of the universe which philosophy contemplates, the mind also is rendered great, and becomes capable of that union with the universe which constitutes its highest good.

Puff, the Magic Dragon? No. Bertrand Russell. No need to reread.

One could translate that eighty-word sentence (unable to be spoken in one breath and based on a questionable premise) as saying that the product of studies should be not answers but more studies. I guess that keeps The Academy intact. Another possibility is to avoid asking a philosopher a question expecting an answer. A third is to beg the meaning of the word 'rendered'.

There is no reason at all to craft a sentence of eighty words except to confound, or demonstrate a mastery of the semicolon, but in defense of Russell, it is often difficult to put philosophical thought into words, especially when trying to give advice, because the thinking continues as the words are being spoken. This can lead to many commas.

That problem manifests itself here as well. It is difficult to advise the use of other-than-rational answers when the advisee knows only the rational approach by experience. Hunches are not rational, but may be correct. Logic and rationality may be logical and rational, but there may be a better way. Since the goal is finding the best way, the problem is obvious. Nobody said philosophy is easy.

THE FUTURE
A MODEST PROPOSAL

You've probably heard that *Now* is the most important time of your life, so let's act on that. Yesterday is history—nothing can be done about it—it's gone forever with the others.

But *Now* goes by, often unnoticed, becoming just another yesterday. What then?

A safe assumption is that you're going to live a lifetime, however long that may be. Maybe it's wise to give it some thought. That brings up the *future*, a long series of NOWs coming at you. With any luck it will last a long time. You can't predict it but you can think about it. Just don't forget about it.

Do you have a plan? That's a 4-letter word to be treated with caution, but the future is on its way and you want to be here when it happens, right? There's a lot of *Nows* coming along called your life to anticipate. Take some time to think about what's being said here.

All this while things are happening. Things to enjoy and things to put up with. You will do both. Things will change. Others will become. With any luck you will grow with time. What will it be like?

Whatever, adapt with the times. Grow with it. It's up to you to do it well. That's my wish for you.

Part Three is about you and the future, yours included. It also says something about me, because it helps to know you're dealing with a person with contrarian tendencies. I hope that you enjoy it as much as I enjoyed writing it.

In Western philosophy (which is not just for philosophers but you as well), Metaphysics has become the study of the fundamental nature of reality. Don't let that scare you off. Believe me, if you picked up this book you can handle the future.

So free your mind and make a difference.

CHAPTER TEN

The Philosophy Of Mind

Ideas

Philosophy

What follows is about *ideas*. A few words about the word are appropriate, An idea is not hard copy–it's a mental thing, the *content of cognition*, if you will. Make it hard copy and is in danger of becoming a *plan*. For the time being let's keep it cerebral.

What's important is that Metaphysics is concerned with ideas, and that's what this is about.

I prefer to look at Metaphysics simply as *the next step* because it gets confusing past that. We are at the point where we must take it, so we ought to think about it. To do philosophy only requires an ability to think, and every one of us has that ability. You don't even have to be taught to think—it comes with the farm. And you don't have to be logical—guessing is fair game. Feelings are valid, as are intuition and insight. You have a mind, and your mind has access to the answers.

Philosophy is the study of the fundamental nature of knowledge, reality and existence. It is the backbone of mankind's intellect including epistemology (knowledge), ethics (moral principles) and Metaphysics (fundamental nature of reality). This definition is debatable but defensible and will suffice for now. If you have a better one, use it. Herbert Feigl describes it, accurately, I think, as *"the disease of which it should be the cure."* Philosophers tend to have an academic sense of humor, but…this hits home.

Metaphysics is an ancient discipline that dealt with the mysticm that served as the religion of the past. By many standards, including published definition, it doesn't appear to apply anymore. It was largely obscured by science, which became the authority of choice in our progress. However, metaphysics remains the branch that studies the fundamental nature of reality. This includes the mystical and the abstract.

Metaphysics has been given short shrift in the shadow of science, which has gotten all the attention because of its success of our education so far, but the need to explore our supernatural nature and explain mysteries that can't seem to be clarified is as old as mankind itself, and sciece falls short of it. We are indeed spiritual beings living a human experience, and mysticism was the historical norm. While science has solved many mysteries, it does not deal with spiritual matters. Perhaps by default, these are the realm of metaphysics. Still, convinced that the rest of the answers lie just around the next scientific corner, we continue to put our effort into the hard science that has served us so well. In doing so we have all but purged philosophy from our operating system, self-destructively limiting our access to a valuable, time-honored resource. Too bad. We need philosophy.

Science and religion have always been at odds because they are in fact totally incompatible. Oil and even holy water do not mix. A major reason is that religion deals almost exclusively with concept (the irrational and mystical), and science cannot. Religion is properly mystical and thereby concomitant with Metaphysics which historically deals with the conceptual and mystical.

But science's dimensions are not enough. We have to explore dimensions beyond the mind, and to persuade ourselves that it's *Ok* to proceed without the proofs and guarantees demanded by science. We must be willing to break free of the self-imposed bonds of the scientific method. How? Beyond the requirement of some level of maturity, it's simple (not easy): just do it. Don't worry about being rational. What's rational about something from nothing? About black holes? Or gravity itself? Being rational and/or logical is not an issue. Getting a good solution is. Recognize that we can be irrational.

Until recently some degree of spirituality was both widespread and fashionable – our founding fathers, in fact, assumed it and employed it in writing our founding documents. Mankind almost certainly has had some sort of "set of beliefs concerning the cause, nature and purpose of the universe" for far longer than our 5000 years of recorded history. Early mystics attributed phenomena such as the movements of the stars and planets to the work of beings with supernatural powers. With the passage of time, and progress fueled by increased knowledge and understanding as early mysticism became more structured and academic. Some of the resulting sets of beliefs—philosophies—developed into religions, each with its own theology and agenda.

But while mysticism virtually disappeared with the development of religion and science, spiritualty did not (because as an integral part of humanity it *can't*), and developing religions took up the slack. Even our own society's conviction that the rest of the answers lie just around the next scientific corner has not persuaded many of us to abandon spirituality. But if science is quantitative and therefore self-limiting, Philosophy is not. Neither mankind nor its philosophies are prisoners of science's logic or proofs.

We have been in the grip of science on science's terms, which include logic and rationality. The rational define irrationality as illogical, unreasonable, unsound, absurd, crazy and nonsensical. Who would choose any of these when seeking a viable answer? But who says that anything other than rational is the wrong approach? After all, intuition doesn't work that way. Nor do the givens. There is no reason to believe a rational approach is the only way to solve a problem.

We should be investigating different approaches even if they are illogical. Mankind in its entirety is capable of everything, and we ultimately have all of mankind's resources are at our disposal, many of which are not rational. Each of us has to work out his own life as it unfolds and invents itself. Doing so requires trust—faith—as well as reason. And no group can dictate what to believe because belief is wholly personal, and may well be irrational. Just as science isn't the ultimate arbiter of truth, neither is any organized philosophy the arbiter of belief.

The function of mankind is to create its world, and that, precisely, is your function as well. That requires, in the absence of sufficient current knowledge, *belief.* And the only constraint, *truth,* You can choose to believe or not but choosing not to will cut you off from what could be out there. And know this: *it's out there. The fact that we are dealing with abstractions should hint at a different approach being possible.*

Are we approaching the limits of science? Well, we're at least beginning to appreciate them. Science will always be with us, even if it tends to mistrust philosophy as impractical. Strange, because it's biting the hand that bred it.

There are any number of intangibles that affect progress that can't be proven. Attitude, feelings and other impacts are qualitative but have an effect just as certainly as those that are quantitative. The analyses of their effects will require a new point of view (POV).

Changing *POV* is never easy—it requires a complete overhaul of plans, shifting balance, and a willingness to jump off into the unknown. Until now we have largely counted on a rational approach, but more and more we find the need to use all of the available resources that we've been avoiding.

Abstractions are always with us. Think gravity. To use them we will have to leave science and return to Philosophy.

It's human nature to mistrust what you can't understand. Robert E. Irving (1953) put it this way: "If you don't understand it, hate it," an axiom that surely has started more than one war.

In returning to philosophy, the first thing we encounter is Metaphysics, which deals with ideas and abstractions. But when we look for clarification we find instead a sea of confusion. Current definitions are anything but clear. A foray into the literature suggests that there are many opinions but little agreement even on the definition of the prefix *meta*. If we want to make use of it, we'd first better agree on what it is. Sadly, often even the experts get it wrong. Ancient and Medieval philosophers might have said that metaphysics was, like chemistry or astrology, to be defined by its subject-matter. Good idea.

Here's an accepted definition *of Metaphysics* presented to make a point:

Metaphysics is concerned with ideas. It studies the fundamental nature of reality, the First Principles of being, identity and change, space and time, causality, necessity, and possibility. It includes questions about the nature of consciousness and the relationship between mind and matter, between substance and attribute, and between potentiality and actuality.

That's a lot to deal with, and we'll get there, but we can't expect to do it all at once. Better to begin with something we can deal with and define it by its subject matter. How about *Metaphysics: The Philosophy of Mind?* After all, mind defines reality and produces ideas.

METAPHYSICS and THE PHILOSOPHY OF MIND

A Contrarian Viewpoint

Philosophy tends to be cryptic, Metaphysics more so. Intangibles are by nature cryptic but they affect never-theless, even if ephemeral. Memory, feelings and other mental concepts affect us as surely as what we can see and touch, and we are beginning to appreciate where they may actually affect the physical world. Witness the placebo effect and consider quantum theory. And don't forget intuition, knowing the truth without evidence or logic. It may just be the way to the future when we figure it out.

Philosophy also encompasses epistemology, the study of knowledge, so basic that it's hard to define. We have to learn to deal with the conceptual and forgo proof. But if we don't need proof, we still need success. If intu-ition provides results without proof, use it. That's where we are. Where are we going? And with what? Metaphysics.

The difficulty is that it doesn't exist–yet. More accurately, the original hasn't been brought up to date. The ancient metaphysics dealt with mysticism and magic where facts didn't matter—one was never on course to begin with. Now we are dealing with truth and the old metaphysics didn't have that constraint, so we are going to have to (re)write the rules. That's a good opportunity to get it right.

Identifying Metaphysics with mind is consistent with dealing with the concepts so long as they remain factual. We are always moving ahead, which requires thought and ideas, products of mind. This way of proceeding would seem to be right on course. It would tend to make mankind more cerebral. Sounds like progress to me.

Methodology

Metaphysics is not super-physics. It's not physics at all. As the abstract branch of philosophy that studies the fundamental nature of reality, it deals instead with first principles, identity and change, space and time, causality and possibility. Therefore, let's concentrate on its *function* as Philosophy of Mind and let mind help *create* the future for us as we feel our way forward. We will make mistakes but mind will be used to correct them as we proceed. *That's what mind does*—Think. And it can think other than rationally. Chances are good that it will result in a workable system, and we will learn as we go along.

Metaphysics deals in concepts—things that affect by way of the mind. Joy, anger, fairness, cause and change are real if ethereal. Things that affect the mind directly, are important and must be dealt with as major items of living.

The spiritual core of life is beyond question. Human life cannot exist without spirit. Metaphysics deals in Mysticism, and life is, if nothing else, mystical, and mystical is not rational. It's time to take on the mystical. To make this major adaptation we will need a new paradigm that can deal with intangibles. Actually, we're already dealing with them and have been since year one. All that remains is for us to figure out what we've been doing and determine what difference it makes. The rationale for this belief is that the history of science shows how the real nature of things often remains hidden to us until it is revealed by a new instrument or breakthrough. The difference is that we will be working irrationally.

The abstract branch of philosophy that would deal with the *fundamental nature of reality* is ready to be invented.

Science is wholly rational. We are going beyond science; therefore we are going beyond rationality. While not rational, it makes sense. *There is a difference between quantitative and qualitative, objective and subjective, thinking and feeling, and between intellect and intuition. Vive le difference. Vive le Right Brain. A different POV is at hand.*

But are we prepared to go with it? Many universities have departments of Philosophy with appropriate curricula in the subject. There are two universities dealing with Metaphysics as well as the headquarters of the Metaphysical Society of America.in Sedona, AZ. Sedona also is home to seven vortices and many commercial mystics. In other words, not many metaphysicists are standing by to provide the needed horsepower for this sea change, and their ability is strictly limited. I have lived for ninety years and met only several, and I am no stranger to philosophy. Those listed in the phone book are largely employed in health and personal services, many in mysticism, some in selling charms and telling fortunes. Clearly these people are not philosophers. Most of them have little knowledge of metaphysics itself, or even philosophy. Those who do are academics, and even they can be wrong. Interestingly, many native Americans have meta tendencies.

The truth is that we are not prepared for a coming metaphysical tsunami. We're going to have to organize to meet the challenge. Fortunately there are quite a few philosophers and other professionals who can be called on to bolster the ranks of those willing to test the waters, and even some converted scientists will come on board as the search proves promising. I am a former geologist converted to philosophy through my work in ethics, and I believe that this approach is warranted, or I wouldn't be writing about it. Build it and they will come from the ranks of philosophers and other critical thinkers including scientists with a suitable mindset. Are you among them?

Why Metaphysics?

Because metaphysics continues asking "why" where science leaves off, and that's where we're headed. It would appear that when we increasingly encounter things for which there seem to be no proof or even explanation, then we need to find some other justification to apply a period(.).

We know that it's mystical. So is religion, which has been around for so long that the two are confounded. But because religion is mystical doesn't mean that mystical means religious. It means rather that the explanation need not be rational. We are faced with dealing with the irrational. Metaphysics has that ability. It is *the* way out of the Scientific Method. Even false answers may be considered.

The future is on its way and was here before we knew it had left.

CHAPTER ELEVEN

The New Paradigm - Mind

Mind, a complex of cognitive abilities that enables intellect, thought, feelings, memory and other attributes that make us human, is our link to the entire knowledge of the Universe because *it is part of it.*

Mind represents our spiritual (but not religious) connection with the Universe, a connection that cannot be longer ignored.

And we have no concept of the many possibilities that exist because of it.

The following paragraph is repeated from earlier because of its pertinence:

Human beings come in three dimensions: height, width and thickness. We take up space. But that's just the box we come in. The real person is dimensionless. That would be his SPIRIT, a *mystical*, not biological, gift like mind, and science doesn't deal with spirit. We do. Intimately. It's what we are—our humanity. It's that unique component of the Universe on loan to each of us that defines the individual. It belongs to the universe and for all we know returns to it at death.

Mind is integral with the brain, where it works its magic and enables our individual lives, asleep or awake. The subconscious takes care of what we can't do for ourselves, and the conscious enables us to be who we are. Rational? Hardly.

The Brain

Each of us owns a complementary dual-element brain system. The left half operates rationally, the right half doesn't. The right half tends to rely on intangibles (feelings, hunches) rather than disciplined logic and the burden of weighing out the pros and cons. It's better at discrimination of shapes, reading faces and expressing emotion. It's time to encourage its help and use what the whole brain has to offer.

Our brains are all about the same size—three pounds of magic—but it is part of the physical body and therefore unique to its individual, the residence of his personal mind. It's estimated that we use less than ten percent of it, so what's the rest for? Well, if it weren't needed it would not have evolved. We either have all the brain we need or less than we needed earlier. Could it contain data , information, knowledge or processing power as we're now using? Chances are that the answer is YES. It certainly is not wasted space.

KNOWledge, the final step of learning, is the goal. (You can't *know* something that isn't true.) Apparently the right brain has something to offer. It should be developed to the max.

Right Brain

The right hemisphere is the thinker's part. It is artistic and sees nuances rather than hard lines, the whole of things rather than individual parts. It is qualitative, feeling and intuitive, more amenable to concept. more creative. *It handles non-rational thought.*

The right hemisphere presents the world as it is, it also experiences *internal* reality as it is. Volition, social cognition, facial recognition, and values all appear to originate on the right. The right brain deals with the intuitive; its use should be maximized.

Left Brain

The left hemisphere controls the right side of the body and is the doer's part. We are historically a left-brained civilization; that most of us are right-handed attests to this fact. The left brain is adept at the scientific line of thought (rational, Objective, thinking) that has served us so well in the past. It is quantitative, more direct and likes hard data. Even our educational system stresses numbers and hard data. It may be tough to break the hold, but using the whole brain is the object, and the features of the right hemisphere are very desirable..

Consciousness

Reason tells us that every cause has an effect and every effect a cause, but it also suggests that there must have been an *original **singularity*** that underlies the whole of reality, whatever that may be. Mankind had been making progress toward its discovery for nearly two thousand years before it was sidetracked by the Cartesian duality of the Enlightenment, which largely purged the idea of spirituality from the system when it threw everything smacking of religion under the bus. But even Descartes's "duality" had to have an origin somewhere at some time (after all, you can't have *two* without first having *one—or can you?*).

Quantum Theory has demonstrated that something *can* come from nothing, strange as that may seem, and that both something and nothing can *be* (not just *exist*) *concurrently*. We now know that light is at the same time both particle (matter) and wave (*not* matter. Could that be the duality that *creates* the singularity?)

Consciousness is not a biological phenomenon, nor is it physical. It is a given, *the* qualitative base, the *essence of life.* Complete, it exists always. The magic of consciousness has many attributes, including spirit, mind, idea, and others like memory, thought, emotion, perception, awareness, intelligence and many other ingredients that trigger the brain when necessary. It is objective in the mass, becoming subjective in the individual soul. When you think about it, it is life itself.

It is the foundation of mind (the most *powerful* item in the human toolbox)—a given, an integral and eternal part of the universe without which nothing could exist. It has no mass—it is not a *thing*. It is instead **THE PERFECT IDEA,** beyond our ken. To deal with it at all we have to go beyond the physical into the realm of the **meta**physical. Strange territory indeed. So what is it, besides irrational?

Mind shares the ubiquitous consciousness that is our link to the entire wisdom of the Universe. Thought is what the individual does with his mind, itself a part of consciousness. The object of thought is to generate IDEAS. Ideas are conclusions of purposeful thinking, leading to knowledge; the object of a working mind is an answer. Knowledge Direct is distinctly different from the scientific method. You can develop it. Everybody has the capacity for intuition. It can be trained. Metaphysics contains that ability.

Mind does its work by way of the brain which is never inactive, and It is the complex of cognitive abilities that enables intellect, thought, feelings, memory and other faculties that make us human. Mind, also called SOUL, represents our personal spiritual (but not religious) connection with the Universe.

We have yet to discover the benefits that exist because of it.

Your mind is yours alone, part of your individual self, but as part of a larger one, it processes information that comes from without as well as what it generates, combining real and abstract data, random associations, unique experiences and every other input, to create an increasingly unique metaphysical structure. The process doesn't follow a direct path from here to there, but adapts with every new connection, unplanned but not random, moving unalterably toward its only goal–more. Neither communal nor predictable, it constantly, automatically and individually just *becomes*.

While we readily comprehend what the mind does by way of perception (sight, hearing, taste, smell, and touch), it's not so simple to comprehend random thought, curiosity, imagination, conscience and other intangibles that the brain does seemingly on its own…

To review: "Mind is the complex of cognitive faculties that *enables* consciousness; thinking, reasoning, perception, feeling and judgment…" (Wikipedia). Notice that mind is not a physical thing, but instead a complex of faculties (abilities, capacities), a function of the brain. What's important is that:

Mind generates IDEAS

The world is a dynamic system that doesn't stop, so we can't stop or slow down if we expect to gain or even keep up. We have no choice.

But so what? It's always been like this in one way or another and, with the exception of the "Enlightenment", we've usually been able to keep pace. Now, however, we're faced with a science nearing its limit because everything it does requires proof, and we're finally to a point where when dealing with intangibles, proof isn't always forthcoming.

Religion has come up with its own answers by way of faith and assumed ownership of the word in their cause. We now think of faith in religious terms but that's not the case. Faith is concordant with trust and it comes gratis with consciousness and as such is a given—we all have it.

And because we all have it we are able to ignore it. It is a given, a constant. But the religious have assumed the term to mean what they want it to mean: faith in a man-like God who runs the Universe.

There is a problem, however. Many religions can't handle the Big Bang because of its age, but instead have fashioned a creation more acceptable to those who created it, fast-forwarding time to suit themselves. Noah's Ark can 'prove' that creation was 6000 years ago. That doesn't mean that it was because it wasn't. The Big Bang WAS.

The point is that if we can accept the Big Bang— the entire Universe being created from NOTHING, virtually instantaneously, then why can't we accept what's happened since then? Or anything, for that matter. If that's the way IT IS, then why not accept it as the gift it is? Since we can't rcontrol nature, then let nature control us as it always has. It will anyway. Relax. It's been doing it for nearly 14Billion years We can learn something from religion—how to have faith.

We will learn metaphysics as it makes itself known to us. The magic of consciousness has many attributes, both active and passive. It is conceptual, massless, yet contains (or enables) fundamental ingredients like spirit, mind, idea, and others like memory, thought, emotion, perception, awareness, intelligence and many other resources that trigger the brain when necessary.

The brain processes the resources of consciousness on demand to think, model, feel, emote, guess, perceive, remember, produce ideas, whatever is necessary to provide the required output or service. Is any of this rational? No It Is NOT..

How Do We Know?

Well, we should know what happened (memory. Science ratifies this by proof. *a posteriori* knowledge) and we're learning more daily by experience and exposure.

But we also know through *Intuition*. Intuition is immediate and direct knowledge not supported by inference, but perceived immediately by the mind. No proof necessary. Non-science. It just IS. Why? We'll find out some day. Is it rational? No.

It is our job to generate *Ideas* to solve problems and move forward. We will need to develop techniques and methods to acquire information designed to help in that effort, The mind will learn to do this as we progress. Using the right brain will help. At the present time there seems to be at least one route into the future—*quantum theory*. It appears to have one foot in science and the other in metaphysics.

CHAPTER TWELVE

You, The Metaphysicist

Ideas

An idea is a thought regarding a possible course of action, which sounds like exactly what we're looking for. There are modifiers and synonyms as well, but IDEA is the primary subject of Metaphysics.

An idea is difficult to describe. it is totally without substance, which probably is the reason for so many synonyms that don't quite hit the mark. An *Idea* is a totally mental thing, properly vague but remarkably exacting. Is an idea necessarily rational? No. It Is *Not*.

An idea is pure thought on any subject. We refer to things(?) like spirit and mind and thought that have no physical substance whatever, cannot be seen or measured, yet perform truly magical functions without having the slightest idea of what they are. They are truly Universal in that they are of the Universe and ubiquitous. Rational? No.

Problems can be solved by way of ideas; therefore Metaphysics is a valid subject and apparently will show its strength when we understand it better.

The brain processes ideas as required to do what it does: think, feel, emote, guess, perceive, remember, whatever is necessary to process on demand input and provide output as required . It will continue to provide information as we improve our ability to understand it by our own thinking processes. We will learn. And we will prosper.

The foregoing discussion is by way of an intro-duction to an approach to solving problems and mov-ing ahead without the rigors heretofore imposed by the *scientific method*. It involves using the resources of the right brain in the realm of the abstract. Is it rational?

Quantum Theory

At the present time there seems to be at least one pos-sible quasi-scientific route into the future—***quantum theory***.

Quanta are *particles* (mass) which are at the same time (massless) *waves*. Not understanding how this can be does not preclude using the ***idea*** to solve certain types of problems, requiring abandoning the scientific method (which requires proof), but if it works, why not? We can't prove the Universe either, but...*there it is,* for our daily use. Nor can we use the Universe to *prove* consciousness any more than we can use science to prove *its* source (philosophy) or words to prove real-ity. We can't begin to explain the origins of that initial something-no*thing* that fuels our existence. *But there it* *is, EVERYwhere, and it is active, everywhere, if only on its own terms. Is it rational?* One point of this appraisal is to demonstrate that even if we don't know exactly what we're doing it is possible to move ahead **on an idea.** And that's what we'll be doing in the absence of generating proof. That's pretty remarkable, better than being stopped in our tracks by not having things go the way we expected. After all, we *could* be wrong…

Once we make the choice to use *every* resource (like an *idea*) available to us to look beyond the physical environment that daily overwhelms our five senses, we can move on, if cautiously. *It is only that we limit ourselves by left-brain rational thinking that prevents our minds from elevating mankind to a higher level.* The right brain can handle ideas. We need to employ the right brain at a higher level.

If it works, use it. Apparently we have the minds to do it. All we need is the *mind* to *do it.*

A (Quantum) Leap Into The Future

The Big Bang postulates *something* (a Universe full of it) from *nothing.* That's some trick. How can we seriously accept it? It doesn't make sense! Again, just do it.

Science isn't always right, either. Until fairly recently our science was based on the assumption that the Universe was a stable entity—then we found that it's flying apart. Have we noticed any difference in it since we learned the truth? Orion's still up there, laughing.

The Universe is B I G, and there's a lot of matter in different forms out there that supposedly came from…

nothing. Something (a LOT of it) from nothing (*none* of it). How is that possible? It certainly is unreasonable.

Well, there *had* to have been a beginning because Reason says so. But who says reason is reasonable? In fact, reason probably had nothing to do with it. But something did. We've been working on it for thousands of years. So far we've found that the Universe is active and B I G.

So B I G that objects in it appear to be in the same places they've been lo those many thousands of years ago. It had us fooled until fairly recently, when we found that they are flying apart at unbelievable speeds. And it *still* looks the same. That makes the Universe H U G E beyond belief.

But perhaps we should first take another look at the word *reason*, which is why we're going forward on all this: "It's *reasonable*…etc." *Reasoning* requires *logic* and *rational* analysis. What has that to do with figuring out something that's not rational? Something from nothing is *magical*. We may be better off with a card reader.

So let's start by assuming that we don't have to *prove* anything, *we just have to explain it* adequately. There *has* to be a beginning. If not, let's *assume* one. Now. What's to lose?

We're heading into the future, and we'd better be prepared to go there exploring dimensions beyond the mind and other very weird things, knowing that it's OK to *dare to* proceed without the proofs and guarantees demanded by our current notion of science. The future doesn't have to be proven before it comes—it will get here as it will without our endorsement, and it will contain some surprises.

And it will be sooner rather than later. We're bumping up against the self-limiting ceiling of science as we know it according to which everything must be proven before it's accepted.

We'd better be prepared for the *Irrational*. (Of *course* it doesn't make sense—that's its very definition.).

Since we think we are a rational breed, comprehending the irrational has to seem a monumental challenge (but we have the right brain to do it). Where do we go to learn about the *irrational?* One source might be those institutions out of society's mainstream where we put savants and other people who don't do well in the prevailing society, yet have the ability to solve complex equations at the drop of a hat. Or count the number of toothpicks spilled on the floor at a glance. Individuals with eidetic memory. Others who seem to live in the abstract. They must know something that we should. Perhaps we should pay better attention to what we've ignored in the past.

Which brings us to the ability to *listen.* Paying sufficient attention to really understand what's being said is not an easy task. Real listening requires total attention without personal thought. If you've never really *listened* (and a surprising number of us have not), try it to find out just how difficult it is. Maybe learning to really listen is a starting point to getting the information we need. And listening to the right people. And they don't have to be rational.

Listening and paying attention are basic skills, but returning to the basics requires some amount of humility and a willingness to simplify.

And we must again engage philosophy. Philosophy (from the Greek, "love of wisdom"), the methodical consideration of reality both rational *and abstract,* might help us into our intellectual future.

Our science has taken us a good distance down the road of finding out "what it's all about,." But we have reached a stage where a new point of view is needed, and it doesn't have to be rational.

There is, and has been for a long time, a competing approach: *mind over matter*. Is it rational? No. It Is NOT.

There is considerable support in the medical field for the *placebo effect,* which holds that an inactive application may actually help a sick person if that person *thinks* it is helping. There is significant medical evidence for this non-rational approach. There have been mindset interventions using placebos to help people reject pain with lasting results, and they are used before and/or after surgery to aid in recovery. Some hospitals implement distraction-based VR (virtual reality) therapy. They wouldn't do it if it didn't work.

The placebo phenomenon hints of Quantum Theory which has rapidly become one of the two main pillars of modern physics (the other being general relativity) since its discovery early in the 20th Century. **Quantum Theory opened the door to the future, confounded science and made us aware of its limitations.**

The theory's principles are poorly understood by its discoverers but have been repeatedly supported by research, even as researchers try to disprove them. This is a case where science studied itself out of a job. They discovered quanta and have to turn to philosophy to explain it.

That's trouble for tradition and the scientific method but hope for the future. "(Quantum theory)... successfully explain(s) phenomena such as radioactivity and antimatter and no other theory can match its description of how light and particles behave on small scales...It can also be mind-bending. Quantum objects can exist in multiple states and places *at the same time...* Rife with uncertainty and riddled with paradoxes, the theory has been criticized(!) for *casting doubt on the notion of an objective reality* – a concept many physicists...have found hard to swallow. "It should be noted that no less than Richard Feynman *did* swallow it...

"Today, scientists are grappling with these philosophical conundrums, trying to harness quantum's bizarre properties to advance technology, and struggling to weave quantum physics and general relativity into a seamless theory of quantum gravity" *New Scientist, Sept 4 2006.* Sounds serious, and probably is.

What has just been described has caused some of us to predict the end of science; it seems to have reached its limit. This is not so. Science will always be with us. But a new door has been opened to philosophy–particularly *Metaphysics.*

Science has discovered quantum mechanics. Any other surprises coming? Don't wait to find out. Welcome the future!

CHAPTER THIRTEEN

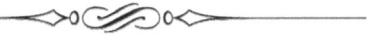

The Future:
Are We There Yet?

You are at the birth of a new AGE. As an integral part of humanity, you are vitally connected to it and the rest of the universe as well. And, space and energy being continuous, it should be obvious that part of that very space and energy resides as well in every part of the universe, including each one of us. That includes you. It follows that whatever happens in any part of this continuum is connected, however indirectly, to every corner of the universe, however large. That includes you. You matter regardless of how infinitesimal you believe you're effect may be, and you do not and cannot know how much or little that may be.

In order to move on, a new POV will be required and yours may be as good as any! It's a new beginning and you are here to help launch it, should you so choose.

It's up to you to realize your relevance and make a difference. How? By connecting, In order to go beyond ourselves, our brains and our minds, we have to get beyond the physical limits that we have set on them and when we do, to assent to an infinite and eternal connection. You simply(?) get in touch with your soul, that individual connection with the spiritual and the cosmos. And you don't have to go to church to do it.

Unless you're willing to move beyond the logical and rational, beyond science and its limited methodology, even beyond thinking, you risk remaining locked into only what you can see. To move beyond that point you have to be willing to go beyond the limits imposed by conscious thought. **You have to know that a verity need not be verified**. *But you don't have to justify it.* Just trust in the concept of spirit and the power of consciousness.

Consider Being Unreasonable - Become A Metaphysicist

Abandoning reason might seem to be a strange thing to ask of an intelligent person seeking truth, but before you make any rash judgments, consider again the surplus of things that we have no way of knowing using "conventional" wisdom, yet must have some grasp of, in order to move forward. The powers of consciousness are great.

Even thought has its limits. We do not relate easily to concepts like eternity and infinity, space without mass or light, the absence of time, or beyond limits imposed by absolute zero or the speed of light. Nor do we truly comprehend insanity. Insane people do not function well in our society (nor we in theirs), so we separate them from us for their safety and protection (not to mention our own peace of mind). We minister to them as best we can, but we can never completely relate on a "normal" level because their "abnormal" thinking conflicts with our own "rational" thought.

Some minds apparently operate on an "irrational" level. But for all we know, the minds of some of those we classify as psychiatric cases (autistic savants who can solve complex mathematical equations at a glance), are operating, to some degree at least, on another, possibly higher level. They know something you don't. Perhaps we can find out what it is. We have to *go irrational.*

Part of our reluctance to abandon reason is a result of an uncomfortable uncertainty. Can we recover? In order to deal with these irrational things and situations, we may have to get, for want of a better term, beyond–out of–our minds. But before we tackle that rather unnerving concept, let's do a little more investigation regarding functions of our physical brains—specifically, the *subconscious.*

The Subconscious

It's a fact that our brains continue to operate even when our bodies and minds are for all purposes inert—after all, brain functions are necessary to maintain life. Accepting that our minds continue to operate at some subconscious level shouldn't pose too much of a problem.

Look up its definition and you'll find subconscious equated with words like mind, self, instinct, intuition and the sublime, even spirit, all essential metaphysical principles of our conscious life—, and all basic to our very humanity.

The subconscious is common to all of us. It's always working, even when we're not. It's only in the realm beyond the rational that the ability to stop thinking has any meaning. And philosophy, in its concern with the metaphysical, should represent a legitimate course by which to move toward the supra-rational.

Humans are the only known beings able to look at themselves from outside. Doing so enables us to develop insight and wisdom not available to other forms of life. This is the reason that we can tap the vast store of information that comes with every one of us at birth. Doesn't it make sense to use these unique powers to investigate our reason for being? All you have to do is stop thinking, and perceive. Let it come to you.

Stop thinking? Now there's a tall order. From the altogether left-brain point of view it doesn't make sense, no pun intended. After all, you usually know you're conscious because your mind is operating–that is, you're thinking. Just making the decision not to think requires thought. Only by being in some realm other than the rational does not thinking make any sense at all.

TRY IT. While it may seem irrational to think about not thinking, that's what we're trying to do. There are techniques for opening your mind to input other than the sensible, many of which have their roots in Oriental philosophies. It requires opening your *self* to the sublime by "letting go." Any number of books have been written on the subject of transcending thought. Some are easier to read than others.

One way of transcending thought is to empty your mind of it–allow whatever comes into your mind to pass through without consciously processing it. No action, no comment, just let it be, and let it go. If it leaves tracks that have some impact on whatever you do or think subsequently, that's not important to the task at hand.

Emptying the mind of thought is not easy because we're so used to left-brain thinking that we are not comfortable when overriding the process. Although not analogous, it may help to consider it in terms of listening.

But emptying your mind of thought and allowing ideas to pass through unheeded goes beyond listening in much the same way that metaphysics goes beyond physics, *and that's what we're trying to do*. It demands total *in*attention, a literally *open mind* and total relaxation. It requires just *being*.

Stopping thinking involves the right brain and the subconscious, opening your mind to dimensions beyond it. But it's not only possible, you can do it, alone. One formal method is Transcendental Meditation, sometimes done in a group, but remember to treat groups with caution. Better to go it alone.

You can do this in your car never leaving the driveway. Turn on the ignition and, instead of putting it in gear and directing it under your control, let it just sit in the driveway and idle. Just sit there and relax, eyes closed, letting the car idle. It's idling, running on its own. It's working, you're not. Let it work—keep your feet off the pedals. Do as I say and you will be surprised by what you may witness. Thoughts will pass through your brain because your mind is working (it never stops). There's a very good chance that it will happen on a thought that applies to a problem that you're working on, something that you haven't thought of before. Creative thinking without any action on your part. It happens more than you think, and it happens because you don't think. Your brain does all the work thinking on its own, and it has Universal access *because* it's working on its own.

After a few times doing this, you won't even have to turn on the ignition. You will have trained your brain to do it on its own. Once you totally open your mind to the dimensions beyond it, you'll have a better appreciation for the subconscious, the subliminal, and metaphysics. Your connection with mankind in its entirety will be enhanced. When you are able to transcend thought, you will make a connection beyond not only the physical, but beyond the mental. You will, in fact, experience an infinite and eternal spiritual connection, as well as a much deeper knowledge of your *self,* which will lead to a greater appreciation of others. *Patience.* It works. Insight to the max.

Trusting in the extra-physical (spiritual conviction) has nothing to do with religion. It's really a very personal phenomenon connecting each of us with the whole of mankind and beyond. Remember, you can't confirm reality through any institution, even a religious one. It takes a living thing to do that, and even religious groups are not vital. But you are.

Trusting in the extra-physical is not-so-simply a matter of taking advantage of the resources of humanity which, collectively, include all the answers. And accept it or not, you *are* connected to the entirety of humanity and the rest of the universe as well; therefore, you have access to all the answers. The Power of One is awesome.

Investigate Transcendental Meditation. It's not difficult but it requires patience and single-mindedness. Choosing to be part of progress carries its own reward.

The Age Of Thought: Mind And The Idea

Metaphysics' signature area of study is ideas, and ideas will carry us into the future. Proof is unnecessary if results are favorable. We tolerate gravity and many other givens without proof.

Where does an idea come from? Who cares? Brainwork is a result of *thinking* and can be thought about further to determine if it is good or bad and if good, acted upon.. Some experience it through participating in mystical or traditional ceremonies, sitting in nature, praying, or thru deep reflection and meditation.

True connectedness is having a permanent relationship with a particular thing, place, environment, or community. These connections help us improve ourselves and others around us. They can also help us view life through a different perspective. In this way, being connected to our spiritual nature helps us reflect on our values, principles, health, and relationships. Spirituality comes with our being. We are spiritual creatures. Embrace it.

Metaphysics provides a base for critical thought by establishing knowledge, truths and values as ontological realities whose nature must be understood to accept its place in educational matters.

Systems thinking is characteristic of metaphysics, and systems engineering methods can be widely applied in metaphysics. The approach can be applied anywhere planning is involved to foresee problems.

There is a real danger in some researchers confusing spirituality with religion. This can, and does, result in ignoring spirituality because of a bias against religion, missing the whole point of the exercise. Man is in fact a spiritual being living a human experience, and it is the spiritual aspect that we are trying to analyze through metaphysics by speculative rather than the observational means employed by science. A systems approach and targeted thinking is characteristic of metaphysics.

Developing the right idea into the best answer to any problem is not a simple task, although the desired answer may appear in a flash. There are many conditions to be considered and satisfied. Now is a good time.

Now is the best time of life. And you are living it!

APPENDIX

A Peak Experience

Where I'm Coming From

THIS BOOK was written because of a life-changing personal epiphany that happened thirty years ago. What follows is the absolute truth. You can believe it or not, it's your option, but that changes nothing, I was totally awake, not dreaming, in complete charge of my faculties and trying to pay total attention and not miss anything. What caused this phenomenon I can't say, but I can say with certainty that it's true—I was there—I *know* it, and my life since that time is the only proof of it.

I was in anything but a spiritual mode when I fell asleep alone one clear and moonless night in a B&B in the Rockies, but about 3AM I shot bolt upright in bed shouting "*It doesn't matter!*" The room was all white light—no shadows—like being inside of a light bulb, yet it was still dark outside. Strange, to say the least...

Why I woke up just then or what didn't matter I couldn't say, but I experienced a sudden clear insight of my place in the universe, instantaneous but complete, that immediately began to fade; most of what I learned I cannot comprehend even now. I remember desperately trying to hold onto pieces of it as it (and the light) faded—it couldn't have lasted more than a few minutes—but I only managed to pin down a few significant points before it vanished. But I can honestly say that I experienced a true enlightenment.

I stayed awake—how to sleep after something like that—frantically thinking and trying to reason with what was clearly unreasonable, and nervously made a few notes. After what must have been about two hours I fell asleep, confused and exhausted by what had happened.

What happened? The best I can tell you is that I was truly enlightened in the strongest sense of the word. And while I learned a lot, it was merely a tiny fraction of what had been revealed to me. But I came away from the experience with a new and lasting appreciation of life that has benefited me ever since, and continues to manifest itself in different ways with time.

After the initial shock of it, I felt totally peaceful—equanimity became a part of my life. Situations somehow became simpler, and as time went on I realized that I had lost all fear. Where the thought of dying had been literally paralyzing, that had disappeared—totally gone. I found a new empathy that had eluded me previously. I felt a new appreciation for everyone with whom I came in close contact—unusual for me. They tell me that I became a better husband, father and person generally. And I found a new sense of purpose. For some reason I was driven to become a writer and a student of ethics. I enrolled in an MBA program. At 60-years of age I'd been wholly changed. I'd had a "transient moment of self-actualization." I'd had a *Peak Experience*. I am a lucky man indeed.

I had no idea of what that was at the time—I only found out years later while researching the psychologist Abraham Maslow. All I knew at the time was that I had suddenly become a better person for some reason that wasn't at all clear. It continues to unfold, and it continues to amaze.

This I *know*: I have been graced with a spiritual appreciation, metaphysical rather than religious, that defies description. At the risk of appearing less than rational, I'll try to describe what's been made clear to me and what I've been able to piece together in the years following the event.

"It doesn't matter!" Why this sudden forceful awakening in the middle of night? What exactly *is* it that doesn't matter? (Begging the alternate question: what *does* matter?)

The best I could establish at the time was that *whatever was or will be* doesn't matter. Things and situations come and go, leaving only traces as they pass through the *now*. What matters is the omnipresent *now*. And what matters is not so much what we *do*, as *that we are*. We're all here for some reason, the primary *why* being that we exist—nothing happens without that.

Mankind will reach its potential in spite of any of us. But this gives us freedom to experiment to our hearts' content, even foul up our own lives and those of others, and it will *still* advance and still reach its goal.

Knowing that mankind will progress in any case takes some of the pressure off each one of us but doesn't excuse our personal responsibilities. These are best served by living the truth. It's all about truth. Life itself is a truth. Truth is the norm–the way it really is, the way it's supposed to be—the primary First Principle. Any doubts regarding what to do are resolved by reverting to truth. We can always return to an even keel by returning to truth. It's universal, a given. We do not define it; it's simply there for the appreciation of it. Not accepting it is our loss.

That summarizes the blossom of the initial experience. What follows is the fruit that came with time…

We live in a reality that we experience but do not–cannot–understand rationally because it exceeds rationality. We know enough to fool ourselves into believing that we can know it all, which keeps us from discovering what's right in front of us. We accept some givens but deny others. We believe that we can work it all out logically. But the fact is that we cannot because it is, in fact, irrational. We can only begin to understand what is beyond understanding when we *know that we cannot know*.

When it comes to the ultimate purpose of the universe and mankind, **it doesn't matter** what I, or you, or anyone thinks. We are inexorably on a path to the future, the length and direction of which we have no clue. Mankind will survive and progress in spite of any of us. The puzzle of the universe *is what it is*, no matter the shape or size of our individual pieces.

This does not mean that we, individually, do not affect its direction or pace. What we do individually in fact has universal effect (because we are indeed universal beings), even if it doesn't appear to affect substantially our immediate surroundings. But, at least in this context...

*What matters is not so much what we do, as that **we are, NOW.***

There is an infinite and eternal unity (for want of a more suitable word) that simply *IS* (rather than 'exists'). This unity has no scale and probably is best thought of as a *point* (a *singularity* having none of the three dimensions we commonly deal with, but perhaps containing more), a source that cannot be subdivided, complete unto itself yet unintelligible, an eternal unchanging *truth* (the principal principle) concomitant with *intelligence,* perhaps even *consciousness.* Everything springs from it. Everything that exists in and of the universe, including its inhabitants, is an *intellectual* consequence of this unity, ageless and timeless, that has existed before time itself (time requires mass in motion, and was itself born with the universe).

Perhaps we can't see this unity because we are inexplicably integrated with it. Our own intellects are *its* intellect. The entire wisdom of the universe exists in each of us. I have it, you have it—it's available to us by (not-so-simply) turning inward. I have been fortunate enough to have been shown at least a part of it. That others have as well gives me confidence to proceed.

So there's the fruit—what I have grown to *know.* You can believe it or not, but that doesn't matter(!). What follows is the jam I've made of that fruit—along with a few other ingredients...

The *Big Bang* theory about the beginnings of our universe satisfies most of the scientific community because: 1) it makes sense; and 2) vital parts of it can be proven. Basically it postulates that the universe began a little less than 14-billion years ago from a singularity—a dimensionless *point*—whereby mass (no less than the entire mass of all that makes up the universe) was created (sorry for the word, but give me another…, how else would one define it?), virtually instantaneously and totally, from …what? **We *don't know.*** Actually, quantum and string theories suggest some answers, but for now let's just stipulate that whatever "it" was had to be there prior to the Big Bang. *This is important!*

It follows that this primal singularity must be the source of everything that follows, both material and not (like our minds), dimensional (how many of those are there?) or not. Further, there's no real reason to doubt that traces of it still exist.

Please realize that this is a subject that can't possibly be resolved at this time. We can't use the product (Universe) to prove its source (?) any more than we can use science to prove *its* source (philosophy) or words to prove reality. We can't begin to explain the origins of that initial something/no*thing* that fuels our existence. There's no standard by which to even estimate it, nor do we know that a comprehensible standard is possible. We don't even have the words to articulate it. For instance: Because of the non-existence of time before the Big Bang (our very concept of time depends on matter in motion, so time in our terms could not have existed before matter), that singularity cannot include time and therefore must be by (our) definition ageless, dateless, timeless and continuous. We could say, for now at least, that it could be eternal and immortal, maybe even *instantaneous.* (Now *there's* some food for thought…)

Since we can't use the terms *energy* or *force* because their scientific/engineering meanings can't be used to define their precursor, it is perhaps best described by the philosophical term **dynamis** (of which energy is its actualization), which will have to suffice here.

It may come as a surprise that this suggestion of some eternal singularity (and its undeniably spiritual overtones) springs from the very science that often seems bent upon proving otherwise. At any rate, we may postulate with some certainty that whatever preceded the universe not only still pervades everything in it (and perhaps–why not–beyond?), but also is continuous within it, existing in an unbroken continuum within and between quarks, solar systems, constellations and galaxies. It was, is, and will be, at least until the end (if there *is* one) of the entire system that contains it. Disbelieving or not accepting this potency doesn't change it (it doesn't matter): if the Big Bang makes any sense at all, so also does the idea that we must be given of it and whatever preceded it, whatever else we may be.

So much for the (quasi-)scientific aspect. There is another. The stuff of religious philosophy, at least in this context, turns out to be no more or less than assigning the *dynamis* preceding the universe to some entity, power, potential or what have you that precedes (and pervades) our world. This singularity is universally continuous from mankind's point of view–a given. It was, is, and as far as we can know, will be—ageless, dateless, timeless, eternal, immortal, all-being *and unproveable.*

Given these parameters, many religious philosophies (along with Isaac Newton, arguably the most brilliant and influential scientific mind of his time—possibly *ever*, for that matter) choose to equate it with an all-powerful supreme entity. (And why not? Consider the Big Bang vs. "creation theory." Darkness must have preceded the Bang, light not being possible without mass and energy. How different is this from conditions preceding the pronouncement: "Let there be light!"? Both require an initial darkness, and what's the cause of the Big Bang anyway? But I repeat myself…)

Are they wrong? Was Newton wrong? Let's just say that you don't know, nor do I. Without making judgment as to the validity of any particular religious belief, it seems clear that for there to be a universe at all, there must at least be some primal potentiality beyond our current ability to comprehend. We may debate its origins or purpose, but it is reasonable that it was, and is, there. *And it is scientifically consistent with the Big Bang, as far as science can go with it*, as well as with the religious proclamation re: light.

So. What does all of this mean to you and me? It means that we are integral parts of the whole, not only in the world but of it as well. We are part of what's happening and, while we have no control of it, we do have control of what we do with it. *It doesn't matter* what anyone or any situation does to us. We have no choice but to accept its being done. Whatever happens, happens; it is our reaction to what happens that determines its effect on us—we can only deal with our response to it. But each of us is responsible for his own life and his effect on others. Each one of us can accept or reject what happens with regard to its effect on us. This means that we retain ultimate control of ourselves. We are truly autonomous, responsible for and in complete control of how we handle our individual lives.

And in order to live right, you need only *be right*. Life continues, time passes, and things move ahead. You can even stop thinking. But *you cannot stop knowing*. And once you know that you don't know, you will begin to know more and more. Let it come to you–you don't have to chase after it.

If you are aware, you will know things that even the highest levels of science cannot teach you, because you already contain the knowledge. Wisdom is a gift, there for the taking if you will only accept it, within each and every one of us, no group required. You can be in complete control of your life, directing it wherever you choose. The trick is to and *know yourself completely* and *believe what you already know*,. It's all there for the taking. That's your project—the rest of it, all the rest of it, *doesn't matter*. Feel free to spread this jam on your bread of life. Or make your own…

That's where I'm coming from. I know not where I'm going…but I'll get there…

Fred L Fox